Harvard
Business
Review

ON
MANAGING THE
VALUE CHAIN

D0823983

THE HARVARD BUSINESS REVIEW PAPERBACK SERIES

The series is designed to bring today's managers and professionals the fundamental information they need to stay competitive in a fast-moving world. From the preeminent thinkers whose work has defined an entire field to the rising stars who will redefine the way we think about business, here are the leading minds and landmark ideas that have established the *Harvard Business Review* as required reading for ambitious businesspeople in organizations around the globe.

Other books in the series:

Harvard Business Review on Brand Management
Harvard Business Review on Breakthrough Thinking
Harvard Business Review on Business and the Environment
Harvard Business Review on the Business Value of IT
Harvard Business Review on Change
Harvard Business Review on Corporate Governance
Harvard Business Review on Corporate Strategy
Harvard Business Review on Crisis Management
Harvard Business Review on Effective Communication
Harvard Business Review on Entrepreneurship
Harvard Business Review on Knowledge Management
Harvard Business Review on Leadership
Harvard Business Review on Managing High-Tech Industries
Harvard Business Review on Managing People
Harvard Business Review on Managing Uncertainty
Harvard Business Review on Measuring Corporate Performance
Harvard Business Review on Negotiation and Conflict Resolution
Harvard Business Review on Nonprofits
Harvard Business Review on Strategies for Growth

Harvard Business Review

ON

MANAGING THE

VALUE CHAIN

A HARVARD BUSINESS REVIEW PAPERBACK

The *Harvard Business Review* articles in this collection are available as individual reprints. Discounts apply to quantity purchases. For information and ordering, please contact Customer Service, Harvard Business School Publishing, Boston, MA 02163. Telephone: (617) 783-7500 or (800) 988-0886, 8 A.M. to 6 P.M. Eastern Time, Monday through Friday. Fax: (617) 783-7555, 24 hours a day. E-mail: custserv@hbsp.harvard.edu.

Library of Congress Cataloging-in-Publication Data
Harvard business review on managing the value chain.
     p.   cm. — (The Harvard business review paperback series)
    Includes index.
    ISBN 1-57851-234-4 (alk. paper)
    1. Business logistics.   2. Distribution of goods—Management.
3. Industrial procurement—Management.   I. Harvard business
review.   II. Title: Managing the value chain.   III. Series.
HD38.5.H37   2000
658.5—dc21   99-28452
                                             CIP

Contents

Managing in an Age of Modularity   1
CARLISS Y. BALDWIN AND KIM B. CLARK

Fast, Global, and Entrepreneurial: *Supply Chain Management, Hong Kong Style*
An Interview with Victor Fung   29
JOAN MAGRETTA

How Chrysler Created an American Keiretsu   61
JEFFREY H. DYER

The Power of Trust in Manufacturer-Retailer Relationships   91
NIRMALYA KUMAR

What is the Right Supply Chain for Your Product?   127
MARSHALL L. FISHER

Make Your Dealers Your Partners   155
DONALD V. FITES

From Value Chain to Value Constellation: *Designing Interactive Strategy*   185
RICHARD NORMANN AND RAFAEL RAMÍREZ

From Lean Production to the Lean Enterprise   221
JAMES P. WOMACK AND DANIEL T. JONES

About the Contributors   251

Index   257

Harvard
Business
Review

ON

MANAGING THE
VALUE CHAIN

Managing in an Age of Modularity

CARLISS Y. BALDWIN AND

KIM B. CLARK

Executive Summary

MODULARITY IS A FAMILIAR PRINCIPLE in the computer industry. Different companies can independently design and produce components, such as disk drives or operating software, and those modules will fit together into a complex and smoothly functioning product because the module makers obey a given set of design rules.

Modularity in manufacturing is already common in many companies. But now a number of them are beginning to extend the approach into the design of their products and services. Modularity in design should tremendously boost the rate of innovation in many industries as it did in the computer industry.

As businesses as diverse as auto manufacturing and financial services move toward modular designs, the authors say, competitive dynamics will change enormously. No longer will assemblers control the final

1

product: suppliers of key modules will gain leverage and even take on responsibility for design rules. Companies will compete either by specifying the dominant design rules (as Microsoft does) or by producing excellent modules (as disk drive maker Quantum does).

Leaders in a modular industry will control less, so they will have to watch the competitive environment closely for opportunities to link up with other module makers. They will also need to know more: engineering details that seemed trivial at the corporate level may now play a large part in strategic decisions. Leaders will also become knowledge managers internally because they will need to coordinate the efforts of development groups in order to keep them focused on the modular strategies the company is pursuing.

In the nineteenth century, railroads fundamentally altered the competitive landscape of business. By providing fast and cheap transportation, they forced previously protected regional companies into battles with distant rivals. The railroad companies also devised management practices to deal with their own complexity and high fixed costs that deeply influenced the second wave of industrialization at the turn of the century.

Today the computer industry is in a similar leading position. Not only have computer companies transformed a wide range of markets by introducing cheap and fast information processing, but they have also led the way toward a new industry structure that makes the best use of these processing abilities. At the heart of their remarkable advance is modularity—building a complex product or process from smaller subsystems that can be designed independently yet function together as a whole. Through the widespread adoption of modular designs, the computer industry has dramatically increased its rate of innovation. Indeed, it is modularity, more than speedy processing and communication or any other technology, that is responsible for the heightened pace of change that managers in the computer industry now face. And strategies based on modularity are the best way to deal with that change.

Many industries have long had a degree of modularity in their production processes. But a growing number of them are now poised to extend modularity to the design stage. Although they may have difficulty taking modularity as far as the computer industry has, managers in many industries stand to learn much about ways to employ this new approach from the experiences of their counterparts in computers.

A growing number of industries are poised to extend modularity from the production process to the design stage.

A Solution to Growing Complexity

The popular and business presses have made much of the awesome power of computer technology. Storage capacities and processing speeds have skyrocketed while costs have remained the same or have fallen. These improvements have depended on enormous growth in the complexity of the product. The modern computer is a bewildering array of elements working in concert, evolving rapidly in precise and elaborate ways.

Modularity has enabled companies to handle this increasingly complex technology. By breaking up a product into subsystems, or *modules*, designers, producers, and users have gained enormous flexibility. Different companies can take responsibility for separate modules and be confident that a reliable product will arise from their collective efforts.

The first modular computer, the System/360, which IBM announced in 1964, effectively illustrates this approach. The designs of previous models from IBM and other mainframe manufacturers were unique; each had its own operating system, processor, peripherals, and application software. Every time a manufacturer introduced a new computer system to take advantage of improved technology, it had to develop software and components specifically for that system while continuing to maintain those for the previous systems. When end users switched to new machines, they had to rewrite all their existing programs, and they ran the risk of losing critical data if software conversions were botched. As a result, many customers were reluctant to lease or purchase new equipment.

The developers of the System/360 attacked that problem head-on. They conceived of a family of computers that would include machines of different sizes suitable for different applications, all of which would use the same instruction set and could share peripherals. To achieve this compatibility, they applied the principle of *modularity in design*: that is, the System/360's designers divided the designs of the processors and peripherals into *visible* and *hidden* information. IBM set up a Central Processor Control Office, which established and enforced the visible overall design rules that determined how the different modules of the machine would work together. The dozens of design teams scattered around the world had to adhere absolutely to these rules. But each team had full control over the hidden elements of design in its module—those elements that had no effect on other modules. (See "A Guide to Modularity" at the end of this article.)

When IBM employed this approach and also made the new systems compatible with existing software (by adding "emulator" modules), the result was a huge commercial and financial success for the company and its customers. Many of IBM's mainframe rivals were forced to abandon the market or seek niches focused on customers with highly specialized needs. But modularity also undermined IBM's dominance in the long run, as new companies produced their own so-called plug-compatible modules—printers, terminals, memory, software, and eventually even the central processing units themselves—that were compatible with, and could plug right into, the IBM machines. By following IBM's design rules but specializing in a particular area, an upstart company could often produce a module that was better than the ones IBM was making internally. Ultimately, the dynamic, innovative industry that has grown up around these modules developed entirely new kinds of computer systems that have taken away most of the mainframe's market share.

The fact that different companies (and different units of IBM) were working independently on modules enormously boosted the rate of innovation. By concentrating on a single module, each unit or company could push deeper into its workings. Having many companies focus on the design of a given module fostered numerous, parallel experiments. The module designers were free to try out a wide range of approaches as long as they obeyed the *design rules* ensuring that the modules would fit together. For an industry like computers, in which technological uncertainty is high and the best way to proceed is often unknown, the more experiments and the more flexibility each designer has to develop and test the experimental modules, the faster the industry is able to arrive at improved versions. This freedom to experiment with product design is what distinguishes modular suppliers from ordinary subcontractors. For example, a team of disk drive designers has to obey the overall requirements of a personal computer, such as data transmission protocols, specifications for the size and shape of hardware, and standards for interfaces, to be sure that the module will function within the system as a whole. But otherwise, team members can design the disk drive in the way they think works best. The decisions they make need not be communicated to designers of other modules or even to the system's architects, the creators of the visible design rules. Rival disk-drive designers, by the same token, can experiment with completely different engineering approaches for their versions of the module as long as they, too, obey the visible design rules.[1]

Modularity Outside the Computer Industry

As a principle of production, modularity has a long history. Manufacturers have been using it for a century or more because it has always been easier to make complicated products by dividing the manufacturing process into modules or *cells*. Carmakers, for example, routinely manufacture the components of an automobile at different sites and then bring them together for final assembly. They can do so because they have precisely and completely specified the design of each part. In this context, the engineering design of a part (its dimensions and tolerances) serves as the visible information in the manufacturing system, allowing a complicated process to be split up among many factories and even outsourced to other suppliers. Those suppliers may experiment with production processes or logistics, but, unlike in the computer industry, they have historically had little or no input into the design of the components.

Modularity is comparatively rare not only in the actual design of products but also in their use. *Modularity in use* allows consumers to mix and match elements to come up with a final product that suits their tastes and needs. For example, to make a bed, consumers often buy bed frames, mattresses, pillows, linens, and covers from different manufacturers and even different retailers. They all fit together because the different manufacturers put out these goods according to standard sizes. Modularity in use can spur innovation in design: the manufacturers can independently experiment with new products and concepts, such as futon mattresses or fabric blends, and find ready consumer acceptance as long as their modules fit the standard dimensions.

If modularity brings so many advantages, why aren't all products (and processes) fully modular? It turns out that modular systems are much more difficult to design than comparable interconnected systems. The designers of modular systems must know a great deal about the inner workings of the overall product or process in order to develop the visible design rules necessary to make the modules function as a whole. They have to specify those rules in advance. And while designs at the modular level are proceeding independently, it may seem that all is going well; problems with incomplete or imperfect modularization tend to appear only when the modules come together and work poorly as an integrated whole.

IBM discovered that problem with the System/360, which took far more resources to develop than expected. In fact, had the developers initially realized the difficulties of ensuring modular integration, they might never have pursued the approach at all because they also underestimated the System/360's market value. Customers wanted it so much that their willingness to pay amply justified IBM's increased costs.

We have now entered a period of great advances in modularity. Breakthroughs in materials science and other fields have made it easier to obtain the deep product knowledge necessary to specify the design rules. For example, engineers now understand how metal reacts under force well enough to ensure modular coherence in body design and metal-forming processes for cars and big appliances. And improvements in computing, of course, have dramatically decreased the cost of capturing, processing, and storing that knowledge, reducing the cost of designing and testing different modules as well. Concurrent improvements in financial markets and innovative contractual arrangements are helping small companies find resources and form alliances to try out experiments and market new products or modules. In some industries, such as telecommunications and electric utilities, deregulation is freeing companies to divide the market along modular lines.

The driver's cockpit for Mercedes' new sport-utility vehicle is produced by a plant owned by General Motors.

In automobile manufacturing, the big assemblers have been moving away from the tightly centralized design system that they have relied on for much of this century. Under intense pressure to reduce costs, accelerate the pace of innovation, and improve quality, automotive designers and engineers are now looking for ways to parcel out the design of their complex electromechanical system.

The first step has been to redefine the cells in the production processes. When managers at Mercedes-Benz planned their new sport-utility assembly plant in Alabama, for example, they realized that the complexities of the vehicle would require the plant to control a network of hundreds of suppliers according to an intricate schedule and to keep substantial inventory as a buffer against unexpected developments. Instead of trying to manage the supply system directly as a whole, they structured it into a smaller set of large production modules. The entire driver's cockpit, for example—including air bags, heating and air-conditioning systems, the instrument cluster, the steering column, and the wiring harness—is a separate module produced at a nearby plant owned by Delphi Automotive Systems, a unit of General Motors Corporation. Delphi is wholly responsible for producing the cockpit module according to certain specifications and scheduling requirements, so it can form its own network of dozens of suppliers for this module. Mercedes' specifications and the scheduling information become the visible information that module suppliers use to coordinate and control the network of parts suppliers and to build the modules required for final production.

Volkswagen has taken this approach even further in its new truck factory in Resende, Brazil. The company provides the factory where all modules are built and the trucks are assembled, but the independent suppliers obtain their own materials and hire their own workforces to build the separate modules. Volkswagen does not "make" the car, in the sense of producing or assembling it. But it does establish the architecture of the production process and the interfaces between cells, it sets the standards for quality that each supplier must meet, and it tests the modules and the trucks as they proceed from stage to stage.

So far, this shift in supplier responsibilities differs little from the numerous changes in supply-chain management that many industries are going through. By delegating the manufacturing process to many separate suppliers, each one of which adds value, the assembler gains flexibility and cuts costs. That amounts to a refinement of the pattern of modularity already established in production. Eventually, though, strategists at Mercedes and other automakers expect the newly strengthened module makers to take on most of the design responsibility as well—and that is the point at which modularity will pay off the most. As modularity becomes an established way of doing business, competition among module suppliers will intensify. Assemblers will look for the best-performing or lowest cost modules, spurring these increasingly sophisticated and independent suppliers into a race for innovation similar to the one already happening with computer modules. Computer-assisted design will facilitate this new wave of experimentation.

Some automotive suppliers are already moving in that direction by consolidating their industry around particular modules. Lear Seating Corporation, Magna International, and Johnson Controls have been buying related suppliers, each attempting to become the worldwide leader in the production of entire car interiors. The big car manufacturers are indirectly encouraging this process by asking their suppliers to participate in the design of modules. Indeed, GM recently gave Magna total responsibility for overseeing development for the interior of the next-generation Cadillac Catera.

In addition to products, a wide range of services are also being modularized—most notably in the financial services industry, where the process is far along. Nothing is easier to modularize than stocks and other securities. Financial services are purely intangible, having no hard surfaces, no difficult shapes, no electrical pins or wires, and no complex computer code. Because the science of finance is sophisticated and highly developed, these services are relatively easy to define, analyze, and split apart. The design rules for financial transactions arise from centuries-old traditions of bookkeeping combined with modern legal and industry standards and the conventions of the securities exchanges.

As a result, providers need not take responsibility for all aspects of delivering their financial services. The tasks of managing a portfolio of securities, for example—selecting assets, conducting trades, keeping records, transferring ownership, reporting status and sending out statements, and performing custody services—can be readily broken apart and seamlessly performed by separate suppliers. Some major institutions have opted to specialize in one such area: Boston's State Street Bank in custody services, for example.

Other institutions, while modularizing their products, still seek to own and control those modules, as IBM tried to control the System/360. For example, Fidelity, the big, mass-market provider of money management services, has traditionally kept most aspects of its operations in-house. However, under pressure to reduce costs, it recently broke with that practice, announcing that Bankers Trust Company would manage $11 billion worth of stock index funds on its behalf. Index funds are a low-margin business whose performance is easily measured. Under the new arrangement, Bankers Trust's index-fund management services have become a hidden module in

Fidelity's overall portfolio offerings, much as Volkswagen's suppliers operate as hidden modules in the Resende factory system.

The other result of the intrinsic modularity of financial instruments has been an enormous boost in innovation. By combining advanced scientific methods with high-speed computers, for example, designers can split up securities into smaller units that can then be reconfigured into derivative financial products. Such innovations have made global financial markets more fluid so that capital now flows easily even between countries with very different financial practices.

Competing in a Modular Environment

Modularity does more than accelerate the pace of change or heighten competitive pressures. It also transforms relations among companies. Module designers rapidly move in and out of joint ventures, technology alliances, subcontracts, employment agreements, and financial arrangements as they compete in a relentless race to innovate. In such markets, revenue and profits are far more dispersed than they would be in traditional industries. Even such companies as Intel and Microsoft, which have substantial market power by virtue of their control over key subsets of visible information, account for less of the total market value of all computer companies than industry leaders typically do.

Being part of a shifting modular cluster of hundreds of companies in a constantly innovating industry is different from being one of a few dominant companies in a stable industry. No strategy or sequence of moves will always work; as in chess, a good move depends on the layout of the board, the pieces one controls, and the skill and resources of one's opponent. Nevertheless, the dual structure of a modular marketplace requires managers to choose carefully from two main strategies. A company can compete as an architect, creating the visible information, or design rules, for a product made up of modules. Or it can compete as a designer of modules that conform to the architecture, interfaces, and test protocols of others. Both strategies require companies to understand products at a deep level and be able to predict how modules will evolve, but they differ in a number of important ways.

Following Intel and Microsoft, it's tempting to say companies should control the visible rules.

For an architect, advantage comes from attracting module designers to its design rules by convincing them that this architecture will prevail in the marketplace. For the module maker, advantage comes from mastering the hidden information of the design and from superior execution in bringing its module to market. As opportunities emerge, the module maker must move quickly to fill a need and then move elsewhere or reach new levels of performance as the market becomes crowded.

Following the example of Intel and Microsoft, it is tempting to say that companies should aim to control the visible design rules by developing proprietary architectures and leave the mundane details of hidden modules to others. And it is true that the position of architect is powerful and can be very profitable. But a challenger can rely on modularity to mix and match its own capabilities with those of others and do an end-run around an architect.

That is what happened in the workstation market in the 1980s. Both of the leading companies, Apollo

Computer and Sun Microsystems, relied heavily on other companies for the design and production of most of the modules that formed their workstations. But Apollo's founders, who emphasized high performance in their product, designed a proprietary architecture based on their own operating and network management systems. Although some modules, such as the microprocessor, were bought off the shelf, much of the hardware was designed in-house. The various parts of the design were highly interdependent, which Apollo's designers believed was necessary to achieve high levels of performance in the final product.

Sun's founders, by contrast, emphasized low costs and rapid time to market. They relied on a simplified, non-proprietary architecture built with off-the-shelf hardware and software, including the widely available UNIX operating system. Because its module makers did not have to design special modules to fit into its system, Sun was free of the investments in software and hardware design Apollo required and could bring products to market quickly while keeping capital costs low. To make up for the performance penalty incurred by using generic modules, Sun developed two proprietary, hidden hardware modules to link the microprocessor efficiently to the workstation's internal memory.

In terms of sheer performance, observers judged Apollo's workstation to be slightly better, but Sun had the cost advantage. Sun's reliance on other module makers proved superior in other respects as well. Many end users relied on the UNIX operating system in other networks or applications and preferred a workstation that ran on UNIX rather than one that used a more proprietary operating system. Taking advantage of its edge in capital productivity, Sun opted for an aggressive strategy of rapid growth and product improvement.

Soon, Apollo found itself short of capital and its products' performance fell further and further behind Sun's. The flexibility and leanness Sun gained through its nonproprietary approach overcame the performance advantages Apollo had been enjoying through its proprietary strategy. Sun could offer customers an excellent product at an attractive price, earn superb margins, and employ much less capital in the process.

However, Sun's design gave it no enduring competitive edge. Because Sun controlled only the two hidden modules in the workstation, it could not lock its customers into its own proprietary operating system or network protocols. Sun did develop original ideas about how to combine existing modules into an effective system, but any competitor could do the same since the architecture—the visible information behind the workstation design—was easy to copy and could not be patented.

Indeed, minicomputer makers saw that workstations would threaten their business and engineering markets, and they soon offered rival products, while personal computer makers (whose designs were already extremely modular) saw an opportunity to move into a higher-margin niche. To protect itself, Sun shifted gears and sought greater control over the visible information in its own system. Sun hoped to use equity financing from AT&T, which controlled UNIX, to gain a favored role in designing future versions of the operating system. If Sun could control the evolution of UNIX, it could bring the next generation of workstations to market faster than its rivals could. But the minicomputer makers, which licensed UNIX for their existing systems, immediately saw the threat posed by the Sun-AT&T alliance, and they forced AT&T to back away from Sun. The workstation market remained wide open, and when Sun stumbled in bringing out a new generation of workstations, rivals gained ground with their own offerings. The race was on—and it continues.

Needed: Knowledgeable Leaders

Because modularity boosts the rate of innovation, it shrinks the time business leaders have to respond to competitors' moves. We may laugh about the concept of an "Internet year," but it's no joke. As more and more industries pursue modularity, their general managers, like those in the computer industry, will have to cope with higher rates of innovation and swifter change.

As a rule, managers will have to become much more attuned to all sorts of developments in the design of products, both inside and outside their own companies. It won't be enough to know what their direct competitors are doing—innovations in other modules and in the overall product architecture, as well

As a rule, managers will have to become much more attuned to all sorts of developments in the design of their products.

as shifting alliances elsewhere in the industry, may spell trouble or present opportunities. Success in the marketplace will depend on mapping a much larger competitive terrain and linking one's own capabilities and options with those emerging elsewhere, possibly in companies very different from one's own.

Those capabilities and options involve not only product technologies but also financial resources and the skills of employees. Managers engaged with modular design efforts must be adept at forging new financial relationships and employment contracts, and they must enter into innovative technology ventures and alliances. Harvard Business School professor Howard Stevenson has described entrepreneurship as "the pursuit of opportunity beyond the resources currently controlled," and that's a good framework for thinking about modular leadership at even the biggest companies. (See "How Palm Computing Became an Architect" and "How Quantum Mines Hidden Knowledge" at the end of this article.)

At the same time that modularity boosts the rate of innovation, it also heightens the degree of uncertainty in the design process. There is no way for managers to know which of many experimental approaches will win out in the marketplace. To prepare for sudden and dramatic changes in markets, therefore, managers need to be able to choose from an often complex array of technologies, skills, and financial options. Creating, watching, and nurturing a portfolio of such options will become more important than the pursuit of static efficiency per se.

To compete in a world of modularity, leaders must also redesign their internal organizations. In order to create superior modules, they need the flexibility to move quickly to market and make use of rapidly changing technologies, but they must also ensure that the modules conform to the architecture. The answer to this dilemma is modularity within the organization. Just as modularity in design boosts innovation in products by freeing designers to experiment, so managers can speed up development cycles for individual modules by splitting the work among independent teams, each pursuing a different submodule or different path to improvement.

Employing a modular approach to design complicates the task of managers who want to stabilize the manufacturing process or control inventories because it expands the range of possible product varieties. But the approach also allows engineers to create families of parts that share common characteristics and thus can all be made in the same way, using, for example, changes in machine settings that are well understood. Moreover, the growing power of information technology is giving managers more precise and timely information about sales and distribution channels, thus enhancing the efficiency of a modular production system.

For those organizational processes to succeed, however, the output of the various decentralized teams (including the designers at partner companies) must be tightly integrated. As with a product, the key to integration in the organization is the visible information. This is where leadership is critical. Despite what many observers of leadership are now saying, the heads of these companies must do more than provide a vision or goals for the decentralized development teams. They must also delineate and communicate a detailed operating framework within which each of the teams must work.

Such a framework begins by articulating the strategy and plans for the product line's evolution into which the work of the development teams needs to fit over time. But the framework also has to extend into the work of the teams themselves. It must, for example, establish principles for matching appropriate types of teams to each type of project. It must specify the size of the teams and make clear what roles senior management, the core design team, and support groups should play in carrying out the project's work. Finally, the framework must define processes by which progress will be measured and products released to the market. The framework may also address values that should guide the teams in their work (such as leading by example). Like the visible information in a modular product, this organizational framework establishes an overall structure within which teams can operate, provides ways for different teams and other groups to interact, and defines standards for testing the merit of the teams' work. Without careful direction, the teams would find it easy to pursue initiatives that may have individual merit but stray from the company's defining concepts.

Just like a modular product that lacks good interfaces between modules, an organization built around decentralized teams that fail to function according to a clear and effective framework will suffer from miscues and delays. Fast changing and dynamic markets—like those for computers—are unforgiving. The well-publicized problems of many computer companies have often been rooted in inadequate coordination of their development teams as they created new products. Less obvious, but equally important, are the problems that arise when teams fail to communicate the hidden information—the knowledge they develop about module technology—with the rest of the organization. That lack of communication, we have found, causes organizations to commit the same costly mistakes over and over again.

To take full advantage of modularity, companies need highly skilled, independent-minded employees eager to innovate. These designers and engineers do not respond to tight controls; many reject traditional forms of management and will seek employment elsewhere rather than submit to them. Such employees do, however, respond to informed leadership—to managers who can make reasoned arguments that will persuade employees to hold fast to the central operating framework. Managers must learn how to allow members of the organization the independence to probe and experiment while directing them to stay on the right overall course. The best analogy may be in biology, where complex organisms have been able to evolve into an astonishing variety of forms only by obeying immutable rules of development.

A century ago, the railroads showed managers how to control enormous organizations and masses of capital. In the world fashioned by computers, managers will control less and will need to know more. As modularity drives the evolution of much of the economy, general managers' greatest challenge will be to gain an intimate understanding of the knowledge behind their products. Technology can't be a black box to them because their ability to position the company, respond to market changes, and guide internal innovation depends on this knowledge. Leaders cannot manage knowledge at a distance merely by hiring knowledgeable people and giving them adequate resources. They need to be closely involved in shaping and directing the way knowledge is created and used. Details about the inner workings of products may seem to be merely technical engineering matters, but in the context of intense competition and fast changing technology, the success of whole strategies may hinge on such seemingly minor details.

A Guide to Modularity

MODULARITY IS A STRATEGY for organizing complex products and processes efficiently. A *modular* system is composed of units (or modules) that are designed independently but still function as an integrated whole.

Designers achieve modularity by partitioning information into *visible design rules* and *hidden design parameters*. Modularity is beneficial only if the partition is precise, unambiguous, and complete.

The visible design rules (also called *visible information*) are decisions that affect subsequent design decisions. Ideally, the visible design rules are established early in a design process and communicated broadly to those involved. Visible design rules fall into three categories:

- An *architecture*, which specifies what modules will be part of the system and what their functions will be.

- *Interfaces* that describe in detail how the modules will interact, including how they will fit together, connect, and communicate.

- *Standards* for testing a module's conformity to the design rules (can module X function in the system?) and for measuring one module's performance relative to another (how good is module X versus module Y?).

Practitioners sometimes lump all three elements of the visible information together and call them all simply "the architecture," "the interfaces," or "the standards."

The hidden design parameters (also called *hidden information*) are decisions that do not affect the design beyond the local module. Hidden elements can be chosen late and changed often and do not have to be communicated to anyone beyond the module design team.

How Palm Computing Became an Architect

IN 1992, JEFF HAWKINS founded Palm Computing to develop and market a handheld computing device for the consumer market. Having already created the basic software for handwriting recognition, he intended to concentrate on refining that software and developing related applications for this new market. His plan was to rely on partners for the basic architecture, hardware, operating system software, and marketing. Venture capitalists funded Palm's own development. The handwriting recognition software became the key hidden module around which a consortium of companies formed to produce the complete product.

Sales of the first generation of products from both the consortium and its rivals, however, were poor, and Palm's partners had little interest in pursuing the next generation. Convinced that capitalizing on Palm's ability to connect the device directly to a PC would unlock the potential for sales, Hawkins and his chief executive, Donna Dubinsky, decided to shift course. If they couldn't get partners to develop the new concept, they would handle it themselves—at least the visible parts, which included the device's interface protocols and its operating system. Palm would have to become an architect, taking control of both the visible information and the hidden information in the handwriting recognition module. But to do so, Hawkins and Dubinsky needed a partner with deeper pockets than any venture capital firm would provide.

None of the companies in Palm's previous consortium was willing to help. Palm spread its net as far as US Robotics, the largest maker of modems. US Robotics was so taken with the concept for and development of Palm's product that it bought the company. With that backing, Palm was able to take the product into full production and get the marketing muscle it needed. The result was the Pilot, or what Palm calls a Personal Connected Organizer, which has been a tremendous success in the marketplace. Palm remains in control of the operating system and the handwriting recognition software in the Pilot but relies on other designers for hardware and for links to software that runs on PCs.

Palm's strategy with the Pilot worked as Hawkins and Dubinsky had intended. In order for its architecture to be accepted by customers and outside developers, Palm had to create a compelling concept that other module makers would accept, with attractive features and pricing, and bring the device to market quickly. Hawkins's initial strategy—to be a hidden-module producer while partners delivered the architecture—might have worked with a more familiar product, but the handheld-computer market was too unformed for it to work in that context. So, when the other members of the consortium balked in the second round of the design process, Palm had to take the lead role in developing both the proof of concept and a complete set of accessible design rules for the system as a whole.

We are grateful to Myra Hart for sharing with us her ongoing research on Palm. She describes the company in detail in her cases "Palm Computing, Inc. (A)," HBS case no. 396245, and "Palm Computing, Inc. 1995: Financing Challenges," HBS case no. 898090.

How Quantum Mines Hidden Knowledge

QUANTUM CORPORATION BEGAN in 1980 as a maker of 8-inch disk storage drives for the minicomputer market. After the company fell behind as the industry shifted to 5.25-inch drives, a team led by Stephen M.

Berkley and Dave Brown rescued it with an aggressive strategy, applying their storage expertise to developing a 3.5-inch add-on drive for the personal computer market. The product worked, but competing in this sector required higher volumes and tighter tolerances than Quantum was used to. Instead of trying to meet those demands internally, Berkley and Brown decided to keep the company focused on technology and to form an alliance with Matsushita-Kotobuki Electronics Industries (MKE), a division of the Matsushita Group, to handle the high-volume, high-precision manufacturing. With the new alliance in place, Quantum and MKE worked to develop tightly integrated design capabilities that spanned the two companies. The products resulting from those processes allowed Quantum to compete successfully in the market for drives installed as original equipment in personal computers.

Quantum has maintained a high rate of product innovation by exploiting modularity in the design of its own products and in its own organization. Separate, small teams work on the design and the production of each submodule, and the company's leaders have developed an unusually clear operating framework within which to coordinate the efforts of the teams while still freeing them to innovate effectively.

In addition to focusing on technology, the company has survived in the intensely competitive disk-drive industry by paying close attention to the companies that assemble personal computers. Quantum has become the preferred supplier for many of the assemblers because its careful attention to developments in the visible information for disk drives has enabled its drives to fit seamlessly into the assemblers' systems. Quantum's general managers have a deep reservoir of knowledge about both storage technology and the players in the sector, which helps them map the landscape, anticipating which segments of the computer market are set to go into decline and where emerging opportunities will arise. Early on, they saw the implications of the Internet and corporate intranets, and with help from a timely purchase of Digital Equipment Corporation's stagnating storage business, they had a head start in meeting the voracious demand for storage capacity that has been created by burgeoning networks. Despite what some observers might see as a weak position (because the company must depend on the visible information that other companies give out) Quantum has prospered, recently reporting strong profits and gains in stock price.

We are grateful to Steven Wheelwright and Clayton Christensen for sharing with us their ongoing research on Quantum. They describe the company in more detail in their case "Quantum Corp.: Business and Product Teams," HBS case no. 692023.

Further Reading

FOR MORE INFORMATION on modular product design, see Steven D. Eppinger, Daniel E. Whitney, Robert P. Smith, and David Gebala, "A Model-Based Method for Organizing Tasks in Product Development," *Research in Engineering Design* 6, 1994. For more about modular processes, see James L. Nevins and Daniel E. Whitney, *Concurrent Design of Products and Processes* (New York: McGraw-Hill, 1989). For more information on the design of financial securities and the global financial system, see Robert C. Merton and Zvi Bodie, "A Conceptual Framework for Analyzing the Financial Environment" and "Financial Infrastructure and Public Policy: A Functional Perspective," in *The Global Financial System: A Functional Perspective*, (Boston, Massachusetts: Harvard Business School Press, 1995).

For descriptions of how companies compete in industries using modular products, see Richard N. Langlois and Paul L. Robertson, "Networks and Innovation in a Modular System: Lessons from the Microcomputer and Stereo Component Industries," *Research Policy*, August 1992; Charles R. Morris and Charles H. Ferguson, "How Architecture Wins Technology Wars," HBR March-April 1993; Raghu Garud and Arun Kumaraswamy, "Changing Competitive Dynamics in Network Industries: An Exploration of Sun Microsystems' Open Systems Strategy," *Strategic Management Journal*, July 1993, p. 351; and Clayton M. Christensen and Richard S. Rosenbloom, "Explaining the Attacker's Advantage: Technological Paradigms, Organizational Dynamics, and the Value Network," *Research Policy*, March 1995, p. 233.

Note

1. Practical knowledge of modularity has come largely from the computer industry. The term *architecture* was first used in connection with computers by the designers of the System/360: Gene M. Amdahl, Gerrit A. Blaauw, and Frederick P. Brooks, Jr., in "Architecture of the IBM System/360," *IBM Journal of Research and Development,* April 1964, p. 86. The scientific field of computer architecture was established by C. Gordon Bell and Allen Newell in *Computer Structures: Readings and Examples* (New York: McGraw-Hill, 1971). The principle of *information hiding*

was first put forward in 1972 by David L. Parnas in "A Technique for Software Module Specification with Examples," *Communications of the ACM,* May 1972, p. 330. The term *design rules* was first used by Carver Mead and Lynn Conway in *Introduction to VLSI Systems* (Reading, Massachusetts: Addison-Wesley, 1980). Sun's architectural innovations, described in the text, were based on the work of John L. Hennessy and David A. Patterson, later summarized in their text *Computer Architecture: A Quantitative Approach* (San Mateo, California: Morgan Kaufman Publishers, 1990).

Originally published in September–October 1997
Reprint 97502

Fast, Global, and Entrepreneurial

Supply Chain Management, Hong Kong Style

An Interview with Victor Fung

JOAN MAGRETTA

Executive Summary

LI & FUNG, HONG KONG'S largest export trading company, has been an innovator in supply chain management—a topic of increasing importance to many senior executives. In this interview, chairman Victor Fung explains both the philosophy behind supply chain management and the specific practices that Li & Fung has developed to reduce costs and lead times, allowing its customers to buy "closer to the market."

Li & Fung has been a pioneer in "dispersed manufacturing." It performs the higher-value-added tasks such as design and quality control in Hong Kong, and outsources the lower-value-added tasks to the best possible locations around the world. The result is something new: a truly global product. To produce a garment, for example, the company might purchase yarn from Korea that will be woven and dyed in Taiwan, then shipped to

Thailand for final assembly, where it will be matched with zippers from a Japanese company. For every order, the goal is to customize the value chain to meet the customer's specific needs.

To be run effectively, Victor Fung maintains, trading companies have to be small and entrepreneurial. He describes the organizational approaches that keep the company that way despite its growing size and geographic scope: its organization around small, customer-focused units; its incentives and compensation structure; and its use of venture capital as a vehicle for business development.

As Asia's economic crisis continues, chairman Fung sees a new model of companies emerging—companies that are, like Li & Fung, narrowly focused and professionally managed.

Supply chain management is working its way onto the strategic agendas of CEOs in an expanding list of industries, from autos to personal computers to fashion retailing. Propelling that change is the restructuring of global competition. As companies focus on their core activities and outsource the rest, their success increasingly depends on their ability to control what happens in the value chain outside their own boundaries. In the 1980s, the focus was on supplier partnerships to improve cost and quality. In today's faster-paced markets, the focus has shifted to innovation, flexibility, and speed.

Enter Li & Fung, Hong Kong's largest export trading company and an innovator in the development of supply chain management. On behalf of its customers, primarily American and European retailers, Li & Fung works with an ever expanding network of thousands of suppliers around the globe, sourcing clothing and other consumer goods ranging from toys to fashion accessories to luggage. Chairman Victor Fung sees the company as part of a new breed of professionally managed, focused enterprises that draw on Hong Kong's expertise in distribution-process technology—a host of information-intensive service functions including product development, sourcing, financing, shipping, handling, and logistics.

Founded in 1906 in southern China by Victor Fung's grandfather, Li & Fung was the first Chinese-owned export company at a time when the China trade was controlled by foreign commercial houses. In the early 1970s, Victor was teaching at the Harvard Business School, and his younger brother, William, was a newly minted Harvard M.B.A. The two young men were called home from the United States by their father to breathe new life into the company.

Since then, the brothers have led Li & Fung through a series of transformations. In this interview with HBR editor-at-large Joan Magretta, Victor Fung describes how Li & Fung has made the transition from buying agent to supply chain manager, from the old economy to the new, from traditional Chinese family conglomerate to innovative public company. Victor and William Fung are creating a new kind of multinational, one that remains entrepreneurial despite its growing size and scope.

Victor Fung is also chairman of a privately held retailing arm of the company, which focuses on joint ventures with Toys R Us and the Circle K convenience-store chain in Hong Kong. He is also chairman of the Hong Kong Trade Development Council and of Prudential Asia.

How do you define the difference between what Li &
Fung does today—supply chain management—and the
trading business founded by your grandfather in 1906?

When my grandfather started the company in Canton,
90 years ago during the Ching dynasty, his "value added"
was that he spoke English. In those days, it took three
months to get to China by boat from the West; a letter
would take a month. No one at the Chinese factories
spoke English, and the American merchants spoke no
Chinese. As an interpreter, my grandfather's commission
was 15%.

Continuing through my father's generation, Li & Fung
was basically a broker, charging a fee to put buyers and
sellers together. But as an intermediary, the company
was squeezed between the growing power of the buyers
and the factories. Our margins slipped to 10%, then 5%,
then 3%. When I returned to Hong Kong in 1976 after
teaching at Harvard Business School, my friends warned
me that in ten years buying agents like Li & Fung would
be extinct. "Trading is a sunset industry," they all said.

My brother and I felt we could turn the business into
something different, and so we took it through several
stages of development. In the first stage, we acted as
what I would call a regional sourcing agent and extended
our geographic reach by establishing offices in Taiwan,
Korea, and Singapore. Our knowledge of the region had
value for customers. Most big buyers could manage their
own sourcing if they needed to deal only with Hong
Kong—they'd know which ten factories to deal with and
wouldn't need any help.

But dealing with the whole region was more complex.
In textiles, quotas govern world trade. Knowing which
quotas have been used up in Hong Kong, for example,
tells you when you have to start buying from Taiwan.

Understanding products was also more complex. We knew that in Taiwan the synthetics were better, but that Hong Kong was the place to go for cottons. We could provide a package from the whole region rather than a single product from Hong Kong.

By working with a larger number of countries, we were able to assemble components; we call this "assortment packing." Say I sell a tool kit to a major discount chain. I could buy the spanners from one country and the screwdrivers from another and put together a product package. That has some value in it—not great value, but some.

In the second stage, we took the company's sourcing-agent strategy one step further and became a manager and deliverer of manufacturing programs. In the old model, the customer would say, "This is the item I want. Please go out and find the best place to buy it for me." The new model works this way. The Limited, one of our big customers, comes to us and says, "For next season, this is what we're thinking about—this type of look, these colors, these quantities. Can you come up with a production program?"

Starting with their designers' sketches, we research the market to find the right type of yarn and dye swatches to match the colors. We take product concepts and realize them in prototypes. Buyers can then look at the samples and say, "No, I don't really like that, I like this. Can you do more of this?" We then create an entire program for the season, specifying the product mix and the schedule. We contract for all the resources. We work with factories to plan and monitor production so we can ensure quality and on-time delivery.

This strategy of delivering manufacturing programs carried us through the 1980s, but that decade brought us a new challenge—and led to our third stage. As the Asian tigers emerged, Hong Kong became an increasingly expensive and uncompetitive place to manufacture. For example, we completely lost the low-end transistor-radio business to Taiwan and Korea. What saved us was that China began to open up to trade, allowing Hong Kong to fix its cost problem by moving the labor-intensive portion of production across the border into southern China.

So for transistor radios we created little kits—plastic bags filled with all the components needed to build a radio. Then we shipped the kits to China for assembly. After the labor-intensive work was completed, the finished goods came back to Hong Kong for final testing and inspection. If you missed a screw you were in trouble: the whole line stopped cold.

"Managing dispersed production forced us to get smart about dissecting the value chain."

Breaking up the value chain as we did was a novel concept at the time. We call it "dispersed manufacturing." This method of manufacturing soon spread to other industries, giving Hong Kong a new lease on life and also transforming our economy. Between 1979 and 1997, Hong Kong's position as a trading entity moved from number 21 in the world to number 8. All our manufacturing moved into China, and Hong Kong became a huge service economy with 84% of its gross domestic product coming from services.

So dispersed manufacturing means breaking up the value chain and rationalizing where you do things?

That's right. Managing dispersed production was a real breakthrough. It forced us to get smart not only about logistics and transportation but also about dissecting the value chain.

Consider a popular children's doll—one similar to the Barbie doll. In the early 1980s, we designed the dolls in Hong Kong, and we also produced the molds because sophisticated machinery was needed to make them. We then shipped the molds to China, where they would shoot the plastic, assemble the doll, paint the figures, make the doll's clothing—all the labor-intensive work. But the doll had to come back to Hong Kong, not just for final testing and inspection but also for packaging. China at that time couldn't deliver the quality we needed for the printing on the boxes. Then we used Hong Kong's well-developed banking and transportation infrastructure to distribute the products around the world. You can see the model clearly: the labor-intensive middle portion of the value chain is still done in southern China, and Hong Kong does the front and back ends.

Managing dispersed manufacturing, where not everything is done under one roof, takes a real change of mindset. But once we figured out how to do it, it became clear that our reach should extend beyond southern China. Our thinking was, for example, if wages are lower farther inland, let's go there. And so we began what has turned into a constant search for new and better sources of supply. Li & Fung made a quantum leap in 1995, nearly doubling our size and extending our geographic scope by acquiring Inchcape Buying Services. IBS was a large British *hong* with an established network of offices in India, Pakistan, Bangladesh, and Sri Lanka. The acquisition also brought with it a European customer base that complemented Li & Fung's predominantly American base.

This Hong Kong model of borderless manufacturing has become a new paradigm for the region. Today Asia consists of multiple networks of dispersed manufacturing—high-cost hubs that do the sophisticated planning for regional manufacturing. Bangkok works with the Indochinese peninsula, Taiwan with the Philippines, Seoul with northern China. Dispersed manufacturing is what's behind the boom in Asia's trade and investment statistics in the 1990s—companies moving raw materials and semifinished parts around Asia. But the region is still very dependent on the ultimate sources of demand, which are in North America and Western Europe. They start the whole cycle going.

What happens when you get a typical order?

Say we get an order from a European retailer to produce 10,000 garments. It's not a simple matter of our Korean office sourcing Korean products or our Indonesian office sourcing Indonesian products. For this customer we might decide to buy yarn from a Korean producer but have it woven and dyed in Taiwan. So we pick the yarn and ship it to Taiwan. The Japanese have the best zippers and buttons, but they manufacture them mostly in China. Okay, so we go to YKK, a big Japanese zipper manufacturer, and we order the right zippers from their Chinese plants. Then we determine that, because of quotas and labor conditions, the best place to make the garments is Thailand. So we ship everything there. And because the customer needs quick delivery, we may divide the order across five factories in Thailand. Effectively, we are customizing the value chain to best meet the customer's needs.

Five weeks after we have received the order, 10,000 garments arrive on the shelves in Europe, all looking like they came from one factory, with colors, for example, perfectly matched. Just think about the logistics and the coordination.

This is a new type of value added, a truly global product that has never been seen before. The label may say "made in Thailand," but it's not a Thai product. We dissect the manufacturing process and look for the best solution at each step. We're not asking which country can do the best job overall. Instead, we're pulling apart the value chain and optimizing each step—and we're doing it globally. (See the exhibit "Li & Fung's Global Reach.")

Not only do the benefits outweigh the costs of logistics and transportation, but the higher value added also lets us charge more for our services. We deliver a sophisticated product and we deliver it fast. If you talk to the big global consumer-products companies, they are all moving in this direction—toward being best on a global scale.

So the multinational is essentially its own supply-chain manager?

Yes, exactly. Large manufacturing companies are increasingly doing global supply-chain management, just as Li & Fung does for its retailing customers. That's certainly the case in the auto industry. Today assembly is the easy part. The hard part is managing your suppliers and the flow of parts. In retailing, these changes are producing a revolution. For the first time, retailers are really creating products, not just sitting in their offices with salesman after salesman showing them samples: "Do you want to buy this? Do you want to buy that?" Instead, retailers are participating in the design process. They're now managing suppliers through us and are even reaching down to their suppliers' suppliers. Eventually that translates into much better management of inventories and lower markdowns in the stores.

Li & Fung's Global Reach

Li & Fung produces a truly global product by pulling apart the manufacturing value chain and optimizing each step. Today it has 35 offices in 20 countries, but its global reach is expanding rapidly. In 1997, it had revenue of approximately $1.7 billion.

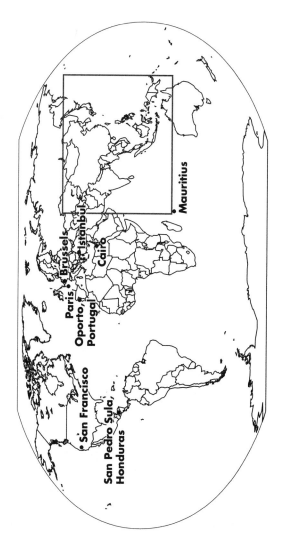

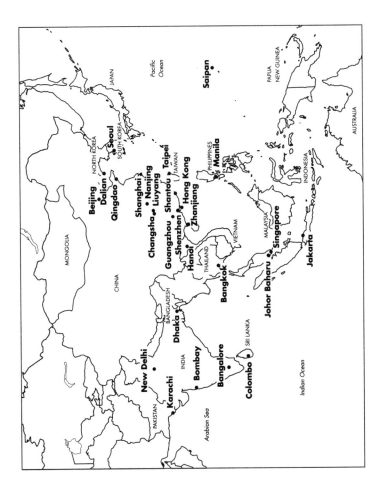

Explain why that translates into lower markdowns for retailers?

Companies in consumer-driven, fast-moving markets face the problem of obsolete inventory with a vengeance. That means there is enormous value in being able to buy "closer to the market." If you can shorten your buying cycle from three months to five weeks, for example, what you are gaining is eight weeks to develop a better sense of where the market is heading. And so you will end up with substantial savings in inventory markdowns at the end of the selling season.

Good supply-chain management strips away time and cost from product delivery cycles. Our customers have become more fashion driven, working with six or seven seasons a year instead of just two or three. Once you move to shorter product cycles, the problem of obsolete inventory increases dramatically. Other businesses are facing the same kind of pressure. With customer tastes changing rapidly and markets segmenting into narrower niches, it's not just fashion products that are becoming increasingly time sensitive.

Several years ago, I had a conversation about ladies fashion garments with Stan Shih, CEO of Acer, the large Taiwan-based PC manufacturer. I jokingly said, "Stan, are you going to encroach on our territory?" He said, "No, no, but the PC business has the same basic problems you face. Things are changing so fast you don't want to wind up with inventory. You want to plan close to the market." He runs his business to cut down the delivery cycle and minimize inventory exposure by assembling PCs in local markets. So what I have to say about supply chain management for fashion products really applies to any product that's time sensitive.

Supply chain management is about buying the right things and shortening the delivery cycles. It requires "reaching into the suppliers" to ensure that certain things happen on time and at the right quality level. Fundamentally, you're not taking the suppliers as a given.

The classic supply-chain manager in retailing is Marks & Spencer. They don't own any factories, but they have a huge team that goes into the factories and works with the management. The Gap also is known for stretching into its suppliers.

Can you give me an example of how you reach into the supply chain to shorten the buying cycle?

Think about what happens when you outsource manufacturing. The easy approach is to place an order for finished goods and let the supplier worry about contracting for the raw materials like fabric and yarn. But a single factory is relatively small and doesn't have much buying power; that is, it is too small to demand faster deliveries from *its* suppliers.

We come in and look at the whole supply chain. We know the Limited is going to order 100,000 garments, but we don't know the style or the colors yet. The buyer will tell us that five weeks before delivery. The trust between us and our supply network means that we can reserve undyed yarn from the yarn supplier. I can lock up capacity at the mills for the weaving and dying with the promise that they'll get an order of a specified size; five weeks before delivery, we will let them know what colors we want. Then I say the same thing to

> *"We think about supply chain management as 'tackling the soft $3' in the cost structure."*

the factories, "I don't know the product specs yet, but I have organized the colors and the fabric and the trim for you, and they'll be delivered to you on this date and you'll have three weeks to produce so many garments."

I've certainly made life harder for myself now. It would be easier to let the factories worry about securing their own fabric and trim. But then the order would take three months, not five weeks. So to shrink the delivery cycle, I go upstream to organize production. And the shorter production time lets the retailer hold off before having to commit to a fashion trend. It's all about flexibility, response time, small production runs, small minimum-order quantities, and the ability to shift direction as the trends move.

Is it also about cost?

Yes. At Li & Fung we think about supply chain management as "tackling the soft $3" in the cost structure. What do we mean by that? If a typical consumer product leaves the factory at a price of $1, it will invariably end up on retail shelves at $4. Now you can try to squeeze the cost of production down 10 cents or 20 cents per product, but today you have to be a genius to do that because everybody has been working on that for years and there's not a lot of fat left. It's better to look at the cost that is spread throughout the distribution channels—the soft $3. It offers a bigger target, and if you take 50 cents out, nobody will even know you are doing it. So it's a much easier place to effect savings for our customers.

Can you give me an example?

Sure. Shippers always want to fill a container to capacity. If you tell a manufacturer, "Don't fill up the container," he'll think you're crazy. And if all you care about is the cost of shipping, there's no question you should fill the containers. But if you think instead of the whole value chain as a system, and you're trying to lower the total cost and not just one piece of it, then it may be smarter not to fill the containers.

Let's say you want to distribute an assortment of ten products, each manufactured by a different factory, to ten distribution centers. The standard practice would be for each factory to ship full containers of its product. And so those ten containers would then have to go to a consolidator, who would unpack and repack all ten containers before shipping the assortment to the distribution centers.

Now suppose instead that you move one container from factory to factory and get each factory to fill just one-tenth of the container. Then you ship it with the assortment the customer needs directly to the distribution center. The shipping cost will be greater, and you will have to be careful about stacking the goods properly. But the total systems cost could be lower because you've eliminated the consolidator altogether. When someone is actively managing and organizing the whole supply chain, you can save costs like that.

So when you talk about organizing the value chain, what you do goes well beyond simply contracting for other people's services or inspecting their work. It sounds like the value you add extends almost to the point where you're providing management expertise to your supply network.

In a sense, we are a smokeless factory. We do design. We buy and inspect the raw materials. We have factory managers, people who set up and plan production and balance the lines. We inspect production. But we don't manage the workers, and we don't own the factories.

Think about the scope of what we do. We work with about 7,500 suppliers in more than 26 countries. If the average factory has 200 workers—that's probably a low estimate—then in effect there are more than a million workers engaged on behalf of our customers. That's why our policy is not to own any portion of the value chain that deals with running factories. Managing a million workers would be a colossal undertaking. We'd lose all flexibility; we'd lose our ability to fine-tune and coordinate. So we deliberately leave that management challenge to the individual entrepreneurs we contract with. (See the exhibit "Supply Chain Management: How Li & Fung Adds Value.")

Our target in working with factories is to take anywhere from 30% to 70% of their production. We want to be important to them, and at 30% we're most likely their largest customer. On the other hand, we need flexibility—so we don't want the responsibility of having them completely dependent on us. And we also benefit from their exposure to their other customers.

If we don't own factories, can we say we are in manufacturing? Absolutely. Because, of the 15 steps in the manufacturing value chain, we probably do 10.

The way Li & Fung is organized is unusual in the industry. Can you describe the link between your organization and your strategy?

Just about every company I know says that they are customer focused. What, in fact, does that mean? Usually it means they design key systems that fit most of their customers, they hope, most of the time. Here we say—and do—something different: We organize for the customer. Almost all the large trading companies with extensive networks of suppliers are organized geographically, with the country units as their profit centers. As a result, it is hard for them to optimize the value chain. Their country units are competing against one another for business.

Our basic operating unit is the division. Whenever possible, we will focus an entire division on serving one customer. We may serve smaller customers through a division structured around a group of customers with similar needs. We have, for example, a theme-store division serving a handful of customers such as the Warner Brothers stores and Rainforest Cafe. This structuring of the organization around customers is very important—

Supply Chain Management: How Li & Fung Adds Value

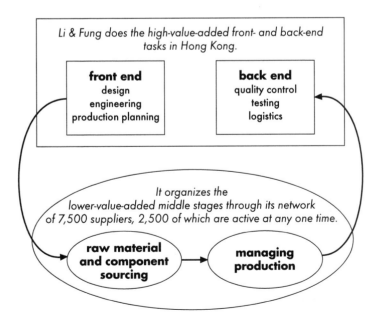

remember that what we do is close to creating a customized value chain for every customer order.

So customer-focused divisions are the building blocks of our organization, and we keep them small and entrepreneurial. They do anywhere from $20 million to $50 million of business. Each is run by a lead entrepreneur—we sometimes call them

"What we do is close to creating a customized value chain for every customer order."

"little John Waynes" because the image of a guy standing in the middle of the wagon train, shooting at all the bad guys, seems to fit.

Consider our Gymboree division, one of our largest. The division manager, Ada Liu, and her headquarters team have their own separate office space within the Li & Fung building in Hong Kong. When you walk through their door, every one of the 40 or so people you see is focused solely on meeting Gymboree's needs. On every desk is a computer with direct software links to Gymboree. The staff is organized into specialized teams in such areas as technical support, merchandising, raw material purchasing, quality assurance, and shipping. And Ada has dedicated sourcing teams in our branch offices in China, the Philippines, and Indonesia because Gymboree buys in volume from all those countries. In maybe 5 of our 26 countries, she has her own team, people she hired herself. When she wants to source from, say, India, the branch office helps her get the job done.

In most multinational companies, fights between the geographic side of the organization and the product or customer side are legendary—and predictable. From the product side, it's "How can I get better service for my customer? It may be small for you in Bangladesh, but it's important for my product line globally." And from the country side, it's "Look, I can't let this product group take unfair advantage of this particular factory, because it produces for three other product groups and I'm responsible for our relationships in this country overall."

Here's our solution to this classic problem: Our primary alignment is around customers and their needs. But to balance the matrix, every product-group executive also has responsibility for one country. It makes them more sensitive to the problems facing a country director and less likely to make unreasonable demands.

Can you tell us more about the role of the little John Waynes?

The idea is to create small units dedicated to taking care of one customer, and to have one person running a unit like she would her own company. In fact, we hire people whose main alternative would be to run their own business. We provide them with the financial resources and the administrative support of a big organization, but we give them a great deal of autonomy. All the merchandising decisions that go into coordinating a production program for the customer—which factories to use, whether to stop a shipment or let it go forward—are made at the division-head level. For the creative parts of the business, we want entrepreneurial behavior, so we give people considerable operating freedom. To motivate

"We think of our divisions as a portfolio we can create and collapse, almost at will."

the division leaders, we rely on substantial financial incentives by tying their compensation directly to the unit's bottom line. There's no cap on bonuses: we want entrepreneurs who are motivated to move heaven and earth for the customer.

Trading companies can be run effectively only when they are small. By making small units the heart of our company, we have been able to grow rapidly without becoming bureaucratic. Today we have about 60 divisions. We think of them as a portfolio we can create and collapse, almost at will. As the market changes, our organization can adjust immediately.

What role, then, does the corporate center play?

When it comes to financial controls and operating procedures, we don't want creativity or entrepreneurial behavior. In these areas, we centralize and manage tightly. Li & Fung has a standardized, fully computerized operating system for executing and tracking orders, and everyone in the company uses the system.

We also keep very tight control of working capital. As far as I'm concerned, inventory is the root of all evil. At a minimum, it increases the complexity of managing any business. So it's a word we don't tolerate around here. All cash flow is managed centrally through Hong Kong. All letters of credit, for example, come to Hong Kong for approval and are then reissued by the central office. That means we are guaranteed payment before we execute an order. I could expand the company by another 10% to 20% by giving customers credit. But while we are very aggressive in merchandising—in finding new sources, for example—when it comes to financial management, we are very conservative.

I understand, though, that Li & Fung is involved in venture capital. Can you explain how that fits in?

We've set up a small venture-capital arm, with offices in San Francisco, London, and Brussels, whose primary purpose is corporate development. If you look at a product market grid, Li & Fung has expertise in sourcing many types of products for many types of retailers, but there are also holes in our coverage. A big piece of our corporate development is plugging those holes—the phrase we use is "filling in the mosaic"—and we use venture capital to do it.

Let's say Li & Fung is not strong in ladies fashion shoes. We'll have our venture group look for opportunities to buy into relatively young entrepreneurial companies with people who can create designs and sell them but who do not have the ability to source or to finance. That's what we bring to the deal. More important, doing the sourcing for the company lets us build presence and know-how in the segment. At the same time, we think it's a good way to enhance our returns. All venture capitalists will tell you that they bring more than money to their investments. In our case, we are able to back the companies with our sourcing network.

One of our biggest successes is a company called Cyrk. We wanted to fill a hole in our mosaic in the promotional premiums business—clothing or gift items with company logos, for example. We bought a 30% stake in Cyrk for $200,000 in 1990. We ended up doing all the M&M gum ball dispensers with them, but the real coup was a full line of promotional clothing for Philip Morris. After five years, we sold our investment for about $65 million.

We're more than happy with our investment results, but our real interest is in corporate development, in filling in the mosaic. We're not looking to grow by taking over whole companies. We know we can't manage a U.S. domestic company very well because we're so far away, and the culture is different. By backing people on a minority basis, however, we improve our sourcing strength and enhance our ability to grow existing client relationships or to win new ones. That's real synergy.

You've grown substantially both in size and in geographic scope in the last five years. Does becoming more multinational bring any fundamental changes to the company?

Since 1993, we've changed from a Hong Kong–based Chinese company that was 99.5% Chinese and probably 80% Hong Kong Chinese into a truly regional multinational with a workforce from at least 30 countries. We used to call ourselves a Chinese trading company. (The Japanese trading companies are very big, and we wanted to be a big fish in a small pond, so we defined the pond as consisting of Chinese trading companies.) As we grow, and as our workforce becomes more nationally diverse, we wonder how Koreans or Indians or Turks will feel about working for a Chinese multinational.

We're torn. We know that if we call ourselves a multinational, we're very small compared to a Nestlé or a Unilever. And we don't want to be faceless. We are proud of our cultural heritage. But we don't want it to be an impediment to growth, and we want to make people comfortable that culturally we have a very open architecture. We position ourselves today as a Hong Kong–based multinational trading company. Hong Kong itself is both Chinese and very cosmopolitan. In five years, we've come a long way in rethinking our identity.

As we grow and become more multinational, the last thing we want to do is to run the company like the big multinationals. You know—where you have a corporate policy on medical leave or housing allowances or you name it.

How do you avoid setting policies, a path that would seem inevitable for most companies?

We stick to a simple entrepreneurial principle. For the senior ranks of the company, the mobile executives, we "encash"—that is, we translate the value of benefits into dollar figures—as much as we can. Cash gives individuals the most flexibility. I cannot design a policy to fit 1,000 people, so when in doubt we give people money instead. You want a car? You think you deserve a car? We'd rather give you the cash and let you manage the car. You buy it, you service it. The usual multinational solution is to hire experts to do a study. Then they write a manual on car ownership and hire ten people to administer the manual.

If you ask yourself whether you would rather have a package of benefits or its equivalent in cash, maybe you'll say, I don't want such a nice car, but I'd prefer to spend more money on my home leave. Cash gives individuals a lot more freedom. That's our simplifying principle.

Since you operate in so many countries, do you have to index cash equivalents to local economies?

Wherever we operate, we follow local rules and best practices. We do not want uniformity for lower-level managers. If they say in Korea, "We don't want bonuses but everybody gets 16 months salary," that's the market.

What we do would probably drive the HR department in a multinational crazy. But it works for us: for the top people, we figure out a cash equivalent for benefits, and for the local staff, we follow local best practices. It's fine if we do things differently from country to country. And remember, we are an incentive-driven company. We try to make the variable component of compensation as big as possible and to extend that principle as far down into the organization as possible. That's the entrepreneurial approach.

As you spread out geographically, how do you hold the organization together?

The company is managed on a day-to-day basis by the product group managers. Along with the top management, they form what we call the policy committee, which consists of about 30 people. We meet once every five to six weeks. People fly in from around the region to discuss and agree on policies. Consider, for example, the topic of compliance, or ethical sourcing. How do we make sure our suppliers are doing the right thing—by our customers' standards and our own—when it comes to issues such as child labor, environmental protection, and country-of-origin regulations?

Compliance is a very hot topic today—as well it should be. Because our inspectors are in and out of the factories all the time, we probably have a better window on the problem than most companies. If we find factories that don't comply, we won't work with them. However, because there is so much subcontracting, you can't assume that everyone is doing the right thing. That is, you have to make sure that a supplier that was operating properly last month is still doing so this month. The committee of 30 not only shapes our policies but also translates them into operating procedures we think will be effective in the field. And then they become a vehicle for implementing what we've agreed on when they return to their divisions.

There are few businesses as old as trading. Yet the essence of what you do at Li & Fung—managing information and relationships—sounds like a good description of the information economy. How do you reconcile the new economy with the old?

At one level, Li & Fung is an information node, flipping information between our 350 customers and our 7,500 suppliers. We manage all that today with a lot of phone calls and faxes and on-site visits. That's the guts of the company. Soon we will need a sophisticated information system with very open architecture to accommodate different protocols from suppliers and from customers, one robust enough to work in Hong Kong and New York—as well as in places like Bangladesh, where you can't always count on a good phone line.

I have a picture in my mind of the ideal trader for today's world. The trader is an executive wearing a pith helmet and a safari jacket. But in one hand is a machete and in the other a very high-tech personal-computer and communication device. From one side, you're getting reports from suppliers in newly emerging countries, where the quality of the information may be poor. From the other side, you might have highly accurate point-of-sale information from the United States that allows you to replenish automatically. In other words, you're maneuvering between areas that have a lot of catching up to do—you're fighting through the underbrush, so to speak—and areas that are already clearly focused on the twenty-first century.

As the sources of supply explode, managing information becomes increasingly complex. Of course, we have a lot of hard data about performance and about the work we do with each factory. But what we really want is difficult to pin down; a lot of the most valuable information resides in people's heads. What kind of attitude does the owner have? Do we work well together? How good is their internal management? That kind of organizational memory is a lot harder to retain and to share. We see the capturing of such information as the next frontier. You could look at us as a very sophisticated IT system. So that's the modern side of who we are.

What about the more traditional side?

In the information age, there is an impersonality that seems to say that all the old-world thoughts about relationships don't matter anymore. We're all taken with the notion that a bright young guy can bring his great idea to the Internet, and it's okay if no one knows him from Adam. Right?

Maybe. But at the same time, the old relationships, the old values, still matter. I think they matter in our dealings with suppliers, with customers, and with our own staff.

Right now we're so big, three of our divisions could be scheduling work with the same factory. We could be fighting ourselves for factory capacity. So I'm in the process of creating a database to track systematically all our supplier relationships. We need something that everyone in the company can use to review the performance history of all our suppliers. One of my colleagues said, "We'd better guard that with our lives, because if somebody ever got into our system, they could steal one of the company's greatest assets." I'm not so worried. Someone might steal our database, but when they call up a supplier, they don't have the long relationship with the supplier that Li & Fung has. It makes a difference to suppliers when they know that you are dedicated to the business, that you've been honoring your commitments for 90 years.

I think there is a similar traditional dimension to our customer relationships. In the old days, my father used to read every telex from customers. That made a huge difference in a business where a detail as small as the wrong zipper color could lead to disastrous delays for customers. Today William and I continue to read faxes from customers—certainly not every one, but enough to keep us in personal touch with our customers and our operations on a daily basis. Through close attention to detail, we try to maintain our heritage of customer service.

As we have transformed a family business into a modern one, we have tried to preserve the best of what my father and grandfather created. There is a family feeling in the company that's difficult to describe. We don't care much for titles and hierarchy. Family life and the company's business spill over into each other. When staff members are in Hong Kong to do business, my mother might have tea with their families. Of course, as we have grown we have had to change. My mother can't know everyone as she once did. But we hold on to our wish to preserve the intimacies that have been at the heart of our most successful relationships. If I had to capture it in one phrase, it would be this: Think like a big company, act like a small one.

Is the growing importance of information technology good or bad for your business?

Frankly, I am not unhappy that the business will be more dependent on information technology. The growing value of dispersed manufacturing makes us reach even further around the globe, and IT helps us accomplish that stretching of the company.

As Western companies work to remain competitive, supply chain management will become more important. Their need to serve smaller niche markets with more frequent changes in products is pushing us to establish new sources in less developed countries. (See "A Tradition of Innovation" at the end of this article.)

We're forging into newly emerging centers of production, from Bangladesh to Sri Lanka to Madagascar. We're now landing in northern Africa—in Egypt, Tunisia, Morocco. We're starting down in South Africa and moving up to some of the equatorial countries. As the global supply network becomes larger and more far-flung, managing it will require scale. As a pure intermediary, our margins were squeezed. But as the number of supply chain options expands, we add value for our customers by using information and relationships to manage the network. We help companies navigate through a world of expanded choice. And the expanding power of IT helps us do that.

So the middle where we operate is broadening, making what we do more valuable and allowing us to deliver a better product, which translates into better prices and better margins for our customers. In fact, we think export trading is not a sunset industry but a growth business.

Was the professional management training you and William brought with you from the United States helpful in running an Asian family business?

It's an interesting question. For my first 20 years with the company, I had to put aside—unlearn, in fact—a lot of what I had learned in the West about management. It just wasn't relevant. The Li & Fung my grandfather founded was a typical patriarchal Chinese family conglomerate. Even today, most companies in Asia are built on that model. But a lot has changed in the last five years, and the current Asian financial crisis is going to transform the region even more.

Now, instead of managing a few relationships—the essence of the old model—we're managing large, complex systems. It used to be that one or two big decisions a year would determine your success. In the 1980s, for example, many of the Asian tycoons were in asset-intensive businesses like real estate and shipping. You would make a very small number of very big decisions—you would acquire a piece of land or decide to build a supertanker—and you were done. And access to the deals depended on your connections.

The Li & Fung of today is quite different from the company my grandfather founded in 1906. As it was in a lot of family companies, people had a sense over the years that the company's purpose was to serve as the family's livelihood. One of the first things William and I did was to persuade my father to separate ownership and management by taking the company public in 1973.

When our margins were squeezed during the 1980s, we felt we needed to make dramatic changes that could best be done if we went back to being a private company.

So in 1988, we undertook Hong Kong's first management buyout, sold off assets, and refocused the company on its core trading business. Later we took our export trading business public again. I'm sure some of our thinking about governance structure and focus was influenced by our Western training.

But I'm more struck by the changes in the company's decision making. Right now in this building, we probably have 50 buyers making hundreds of individual transactions. We're making a large number of small decisions instead of a small number of big ones. I can't be involved in all of them. So today I depend on structure, on guiding principles, on managing a system.

Of course, I think relationships are still important, but I'm not managing a single key relationship and using it to leverage my entire enterprise. Instead, I'm running a very focused business using a systems approach. That's why I say that in the last five years, everything I learned in business school has come to matter.

Li & Fung is a good example of the new generation of companies coming out of Asia. As the currency crisis destroys the old model, stronger companies will emerge from the ashes, still bolstered by Asia's strong work ethic and high savings rates, but more narrowly focused and professionally run by what we can call the "M.B.A. sons."

What's driving Hong Kong is a large number—about 300,000—of small and midsize enterprises. About 40% of those companies are transnational; that is, they operate in two or more territories. Some may have 20 to 30 people in Hong Kong, plus a factory in mainland China with 200 or 300 people. Hong Kong runs about 50,000 factories in southern China, employing about 5 million workers. Hong Kong is producing a new breed of company. I don't think there will be many the size of General

Motors or AT&T. But there will be lots of very focused companies that will break into the *Fortune* 1,000. I hope Li & Fung is one of them.

A Tradition of Innovation

IN THE COMPANY'S early years, Li & Fung dealt in porcelain and other traditional Chinese products, including bamboo and rattan ware, jade and ivory handicrafts—and fireworks. Li & Fung's invention of paper-sealed firecrackers in 1907 to replace the traditional mud-sealed firecracker was a major breakthrough. At that time, the U.S. import duty on firecrackers was based on weight. The paper-sealed firecrackers not only incurred lower import duties by being lighter but also eliminated the problem of excessive dust produced by the discharge of the mud-sealed variety. Li & Fung's paper-sealed manufacturing process has become the industry's standard.

Originally published in September–October 1998
Reprint 98507

How Chrysler Created an
American Keiretsu

JEFFREY H. DYER

Executive Summary

MANY U.S. MANAGERS WANT to enlist their suppliers in their efforts to develop products faster and to reduce manufacturing costs. But they have wondered whether they can have the sort of mutually supportive relationship that characterizes manufacturers and suppliers in a Japanese keiretsu. Chrysler Corporation shows that the model can indeed be adapted successfully.

Chrysler's relationship with its suppliers used to be one of mutual distrust and suspicion. The automaker chose suppliers primarily on their ability to build components at the lowest possible cost. It did not consult with them about the design of the components, and it considered their profit margins to be none of its concern. At the end of the 1980s, however, dire financial straits convinced the company that it had to rethink its supplier relations. The resulting new model has played a major role in Chrysler's stunning revival.

Critical components of the model include cross-functional teams, target costing, choosing suppliers early in the vehicle's concept-development stage, and having Chrysler's and its suppliers' engineers work side by side to develop components. But in many ways, Chrysler's SCORE program is the heart of the model. SCORE has helped Chrysler involve suppliers deeply in the company's efforts to lower costs and make processes more efficient. Whereas Chrysler once ignored suppliers' money-saving ideas, it now solicits them—and shares the savings. For Chrysler, the result has been annual savings of more than $1.7 billion. The automaker has proved that highly productive partnerships with suppliers not only can flourish in the United States but are the wave of the future.

BORROWING FROM JAPANESE practices, U.S. manufacturers have cut their production and component costs dramatically in the last decade by overhauling their supplier bases. They have radically pruned the ranks of their suppliers and given more work to the survivors in return for lower prices. And by getting their remaining suppliers to deliver parts just in time and to take responsibility for quality, they have managed to slash inventories, reduce defects, and greatly improve the efficiency of their own production lines.

Now many manufacturers are striving to wring even greater benefits from their suppliers. They would like to involve suppliers much more deeply in product development and to enlist them in the drive for continual improvements of production processes. The prizes they are seeking: ever more innovative products, ever faster product development, and ever lower costs.

But as many managers now realize, accomplishing the first stage was relatively easy because it did not require altering the nature of their relationship with suppliers. The traditional adversarial relationship remained: Manufacturers continued to design products largely without input from suppliers, to pick suppliers on the basis of price through a competitive bidding process, and to dictate the detailed terms of the contract. They continued to expect suppliers to do as they were told and not much more.

In sharp contrast, the second stage—involving suppliers in product development and process improvement—requires radically changing the nature of the relationship. It requires a bona fide partnership, in which there is an unimpeded two-way flow of ideas. Although many managers now talk about their desire to turn their suppliers into partners, the fact of the matter is that actually doing it—after decades of exploiting suppliers by pitting one against the other—is exceedingly difficult. Indeed, the task is so difficult that some executives wonder whether the Japanese partnership model can or even should be transplanted to the United States, where competitive, contractual, arm's-length relationships between manufacturers and their suppliers have long been the norm. They rightly point out that the partnerships among the members of a Japanese keiretsu grew out of cultural and historical experiences that are very different from those that shaped U.S. industries and companies.

One U.S. manufacturer, however, has shown that it is possible to make the transition. This company is Chrysler Corporation. Its experience demonstrates not only that a modified form of the keiretsu model can work in the United States but also that the benefits can be enormous.

Since 1989, Chrysler has shrunk its production supplier base from 2,500 companies to 1,140 and has fundamentally changed the way it works with those that remain. Instead of forcing suppliers to win its business anew every two years, Chrysler now gives most of them business for the life of a model and beyond; excruciatingly detailed contracts have given way to oral agreements. Instead of relying solely on its own engineers to create the concept for a new car and then to design all the car's components, Chrysler now involves suppliers deeply. And instead of Chrysler dictating prices to suppliers, regardless of whether the prices are realistic or fair, the two sides now strive *together* to find ways to lower the costs of making cars and to share the savings.

The results have been astounding. The time Chrysler needs to develop a new vehicle is approaching 160 weeks, down from an average of 234 weeks during the 1980s. The cost of developing a new vehicle has plunged an estimated 20% to 40% during the last decade to less than $1 billion for the Cirrus/Stratus, introduced this year. And, at the same time, Chrysler has managed to produce one consumer hit after another—including the Neon, the Dodge Ram truck, the Cirrus/Stratus, and the new minivan (sold as the Town & Country, Dodge Caravan, and Plymouth Voyager). As a result, Chrysler's profit per vehicle has jumped from an average of $250 in the 1980s to a record (for all U.S. automakers) of $2,110 in 1994. (See the "How Supplier Partnerships Helped Revive Chrysler" at the end of this article.)

Chrysler came to realize that trust takes root only if suppliers share the rewards, not just the risks.

Of course, Chrysler's astounding comeback is hardly news anymore. But surprisingly, one crucial aspect of the story has been overlooked: exactly how the company managed to transform its contentious relationships with its suppliers. Believing that Chrysler's turnaround might hold lessons for other U.S. manufacturers, I undertook a three-year study of the company's revival. From 1993 to 1996, I interviewed 13 executives at Chrysler and also 33 of the company's suppliers, and analyzed thousands of pages of Chrysler's documents.

From this work emerged a blueprint of the steps that other companies might take to build their own American keiretsus, providing that those steps are accompanied by the exemplary management—or, more accurately, the exemplary leadership—that Chrysler's executives displayed. Four men in particular—Robert Lutz, Chrysler's president; François Castaing, the head of vehicle engineering; Glenn Gardner, LH program manager; and Thomas Stallkamp, head of purchasing, planted the seeds and then nurtured Chrysler's keiretsu. By benchmarking competitors, listening to suppliers, and experimenting with ideas and programs, they gradually developed a vision of the changes that Chrysler needed to make. They came to realize that those changes required transforming both the process of choosing and working with suppliers and the personal relationships between Chrysler's staff and its suppliers. They came to understand that people—both at Chrysler and in suppliers' organizations—must have a common vision of how to collaborate to create value jointly. They came to recognize that trust in relationships will take root only if both parties share in the rewards and not just the risks. And ultimately they incorporated those realizations into the fabric of the company's management systems.

To be candid, the steps that Chrysler took were not always by design. But through trial and error, the automaker has managed to develop supplier management practices that are a model of cooperation and efficiency.

The Impetus for Change

In the mid-1980s, as part of an effort to improve its competitiveness, Chrysler conducted an extensive benchmarking study of product development and manufacturing at Honda Motor Company, which was then expanding its manufacturing and sales presence in the United States faster than either Toyota Motor Corporation or Nissan Motor Company. One factor that Chrysler studied was supplier relations.

Honda was organized into product development teams composed of individuals from all key functions, all of whom had cradle-to-grave responsibility for the development of a vehicle. The teams included suppliers' engineers, who had responsibility for both the design and manufacture of a particular component or system. Executives from Chrysler thought initially that Honda's practices were interesting but completely foreign to Chrysler, which was organized by function and which developed products in a traditional sequential process that did not routinely involve suppliers. Chrysler's engineers designed components, and suppliers built them. Whereas Honda selected suppliers that had a history of good relations with the company and a track record for delivering quality products and meeting cost targets, Chrysler selected suppliers that could build components at the lowest possible cost. (Buyers had to obtain quotations from at least three suppliers.) A supplier's track record for performance and quality was relatively unimportant. As a consequence, the typical relationship between Chrysler and its suppliers was characterized by mutual distrust and suspicion.

Honda's approach suddenly looked less foreign after Chrysler acquired the American Motors Corporation in 1987 for its profitable Jeep operations. AMC had implemented some Honda-like supplier-management and development practices. The reason was necessity. Because AMC had neither the resources to design all its own parts nor the power of larger automakers to dictate the prices it was willing to pay for them, it had learned to rely on suppliers to engineer and design a number of its vehicles' components. Also, the engineering and manufacturing staff in AMC's Jeep and truck group had been operating for several years as an integrated team. With just 1,000 engineering employees, AMC had developed three vehicles between 1980 and 1987—the Cherokee, the Premier, and the Comanche—and was beginning a fourth, the Allure coupe. In comparison, Chrysler's 5,500 engineers and technicians had developed only four all-new vehicles during the 1980s: the K-car, the minivan, the Dakota truck, and the Shadow/Sundance.

AMC's operations suggested to Chrysler's executives that Japanese-style partnerships might be possible in an American context. Equally important, that discovery occurred at a time when Chrysler's leaders had been made keenly aware that their development process was inadequate. The company's newly

Lutz championed the effort to adapt and apply the lessons learned from Honda and AMC.

launched LH program (Chrysler Concord, Eagle Vision, and Dodge Intrepid—Chrysler's answers to Ford Motor

Company's popular Taurus) was running a projected
$1 billion over budget, and the company was in dire
financial straits. It had a $4.5 billion unfunded pension
fund. Its losses were deepening: after closing three plants
in 18 months during 1988 and 1989, Chrysler hit bottom,
reporting a record loss of $664 million in the fourth quar-
ter of 1989. With the exception of the minivan, its boxy
cars appealed only to older buyers. Chrysler's executives
knew they had to do something fast.

Some changes in top management helped. Lutz, who
had become president of operations in 1988, championed
the effort to adapt and apply the positive lessons learned
from Honda and AMC. When Chrysler's chief engineer
retired in 1988, Lutz replaced him with François Castaing,
AMC's chief engineer. In one of his first moves, Castaing
recommended that Chrysler slam the brakes on the LH
program, and the company picked Glenn Gardner to rethink and relaunch the program. Gardner had been chairman of Diamond-Star Motors Corporation, Chrysler's
joint venture with Mitsubishi Motors Corporation, and
was familiar with Mitsubishi's product-development process, which was similar to Honda's.

Lutz, Castaing, and Gardner picked the team to
develop the LH, a model code that many at Chrysler
darkly joked stood for "last hope." The reborn LH program was to serve as a pilot for redesigning Chrysler's
product-development process and supplier relations.

To spur creativity and increase the speed of the product development cycle, the three executives made three
important changes that broke with tradition. First, to
shield the team from internal bureaucracy, they decided
to move it away from Highland Park, Michigan, where
most of Chrysler's operations were located. Second, to
speed decisions internally and to eliminate sequential

decision making, they included on the team individuals from design, engineering, manufacturing, procurement, marketing, and finance. Finally, they decided to experiment with new methods of working with suppliers, drawing on the lessons learned from Honda, AMC, and Mitsubishi. (See the exhibit "Supplier-Management Practices at Chrysler Have Changed.")

By 1991, Chrysler's senior managers knew they were onto something. The LH was being developed in record time and below the aggressive cost targets set at the beginning of the program. The new approach to product development and working with suppliers was extended to the rest of the company that year.

Chrysler's New Model

The model of supplier management that Chrysler now uses reflects several important changes in the company's processes for selecting, working with, and evaluating suppliers.

CROSS-FUNCTIONAL TEAMS

To get its functions to present one face to suppliers and to end the conflicting demands and shifting priorities that had been the hallmark of its sequential development process, the company reorganized into cross-functional vehicle-development teams. It now has five cross-functional platform teams—one for large cars, one for small cars, one for minivans, one for Jeeps, and one for trucks.

The rationale for presourcing is that it lets many engineering tasks be carried out simultaneously.

Cross-functional teams improve continuity, coordination, and trust both within Chrysler and between Chrysler and its suppliers. Suppliers also develop more stable relationships with Chrysler's staff and can count on the company to follow through more effectively on promises and agreements.

PRESOURCING AND TARGET COSTING

Presourcing means choosing suppliers early in the vehicle's concept-development stage and giving them significant, if not total, responsibility for designing a given component or system. The rationale for presourcing is that it permits many engineering tasks to be carried out simultaneously rather than sequentially, thereby speeding up the development process.

In addition to having responsibility for design, most presourced suppliers are responsible for building prototypes during development and for manufacturing the component or system in volume once the vehicle is in commercial production. The new practice means that suppliers of such complex components as the heating and air-conditioning system join the product development effort very early and, as prime contractors, take total responsibility for the cost, quality, and on-time delivery of their systems. Suppliers say this approach gives them more flexibility in developing effective solutions to problems.

In the past, Chrysler had often given responsibility for design, manufacture of prototypes, and volume production of a component to separate companies, with the result being a lack of accountability. When suppliers had problems producing a component at the required cost or quality, they would often blame their troubles on the design—not surprising, given that some studies have found that 70% of quality problems in automotive components are due to poor design. Consequently, Chrysler and its suppliers would waste time trying to assign blame for problems when they could have been trying to solve them.

To overcome that fragmented approach, Chrysler had to move away from competitive bidding. For the LH

Supplier-Management Practices at Chrysler Have Changed

Process Characteristics		Relational Characteristics	
1989	**1994**	**1989**	**1994**
Suppliers chosen by competitive bid • Low price wins • Selection after design	Suppliers presourced • Cost targeted to a set price • Selection before design, based on capabilities	Little recognition or credit for past performance (transaction orientation)	Recognition of past performance and track record (relationship orientation)
Split accountability for design, prototype, and production parts	Single supplier accountable for design, prototype, and production parts	No responsibility for suppliers' profit margins	Recognition of suppliers' need to make a fair profit
Minimal supplier investment in coordination mechanisms and dedicated assets	Substantial investments in coordination mechanisms and dedicated assets	Little support for feedback from suppliers	Feedback from suppliers encouraged
Discrete activity focus; no process for soliciting ideas or suggestions	Focus on total value-chain improvement; formal process for soliciting suppliers' suggestions	No guarantee of business relationship beyond the contract	Expectation of business relationship beyond the contract
Simple performance evaluation	Complex performance evaluation	No performance expectations beyond the contract	Considerable performance expectations beyond the contract
Short-term contracts	Long-term contracts	Adversarial, zero-sum game	Cooperative and trusting

project, Chrysler's corporate purchasing department gave the project's cross-functional platform team a pre-qualified list of suppliers considered to have the most advanced engineering and manufacturing capabilities. That team, which included people from engineering, quality control, and purchasing, then selected suppliers on the basis of proven ability to design and manufacture the component or system. Each supplier's success in meeting design, cost, and quality targets and in delivering on time was critical to the success of the presourcing process.

The new process also required Chrysler to decide how to set a fair price for the component. Under the old competitive-bidding process, the price of a component or system was deemed fair because it was market driven. However, under the new system, Chrysler had to choose the supplier even before the component was designed. Chrysler decided to adopt the widely used Japanese practice of *target costing*, which involves determining what price the market, or end customer, will pay for the vehicle and then working backward to calculate the allowable costs for systems, subsystems, and components.

How did the company set the initial target costs in the LH program? "Actually, we set them somewhat unscientifically and then, when necessary, had the suppliers convince us that another number was better," says Barry Price, Chrysler's executive director of platform supply for procurement and supply. "We would involve suppliers and tell them, 'I've got X amount of money.' We would let them know what functions the part or system in question would be required to perform and ask, 'Can you supply it for that cost?' Usually, their response would be no, but they at least came back with some alternatives. The first time through, we had to find our way. The second time, we had the benefit of history and, as a result, we developed better targets at the outset of the program."

Target costing has shifted Chrysler's relationship with suppliers from a zero-sum game to a positive-sum game. Historically, Chrysler had put constant pressure on suppliers to reduce prices, regardless of whether the suppliers had been able to reduce costs; the automaker did not feel responsible for ensuring that suppliers made a reasonable profit. Chrysler's new focus on cost instead of price has created a win-win situation with suppliers because the company works *with* suppliers to meet common cost and functional objectives. Naturally, this process begins to build the trust that is critical if partnerships are to take root.

TOTAL VALUE-CHAIN IMPROVEMENT: THE SCORE PROGRAM

The next step in building a partnership with suppliers is to figure out how to motivate them to participate in continuous improvement processes for the value chain as a whole. Eliciting the full effort and total resources of suppliers is critical because partnerships work only when both parties try to expand the pie. Such cooperation is possible only when the supplier trusts the buyer and when the two parties *really* communicate.

Chrysler began to build trust and improve communications with a small set of suppliers during the reborn LH program. However, it was another program, one that Chrysler began to develop in 1989, that became, almost by accident, the company's most important method for building trust, lowering costs, and improving communication. The formal name of that program now is the Supplier Cost Reduction Effort (dubbed SCORE).

Asking for help.   The basic purpose of SCORE is to help suppliers and Chrysler reduce systemwide costs without hurting suppliers' profits. The catalyst for the SCORE program was a speech that Lutz gave at the Detroit Athletic Club in August 1989 to executives from 25 of Chrysler's largest suppliers. Lutz told the suppliers that because of Chrysler's desperate situation, he wanted their assistance and ideas on how the company could lower both its own costs and those of its suppliers. The message was, "All I want is your brainpower, not your margins."

The fledgling efforts in the LH program to build tighter relationships with suppliers were bearing fruit, and Chrysler's leaders were eager to maintain the momentum. At the time, General Motors Corporation was increasing its squeeze on suppliers, demanding across-the-board price cuts. In his speech, Lutz wanted to stress that Chrysler was taking a different path.

The suppliers crowded around Lutz after the speech, eager to offer their ideas. Given Chrysler's history of adversarial relationships with suppliers, one might ask why they didn't react cynically to Lutz's request for help. For one thing, they knew that Chrysler was on the ropes. For another, Chrysler had four relatively new leaders who had demonstrated a commitment to radical change: Lutz, Castaing, Gardner, and Stallkamp, the purchasing chief who, in early 1990, had replaced a champion of competitive bidding. There also was hard evidence of Chrysler's sincerity: AMC and the relaunched LH program.

Lutz kept the ball rolling after the speech. He was so impressed with the suppliers' ideas and willingness to share information that he had senior executives schedule follow-up meetings with them. Some ideas were so good that Lutz, Castaing, and Stallkamp decided to establish a formal process for reviewing, approving, and implementing them.

To get advice on how Chrysler could accomplish that task more systematically, Lutz asked a small group of Chrysler's senior executives, including Castaing and Stallkamp, to visit a number of key suppliers. These unusual visits impressed the suppliers, many of whom were upset with GM's heavy-handed treatment. (Chrysler would later strive to contrast its approach with GM's in order to drive home the point that Chrysler's path was different. For example, at a time when GM's purchasing czar, Jose Ignacio Lopez, was prohibiting his buyers from accepting a lunch invitation from a supplier, Stallkamp was instructing his buyers to take suppliers to lunch.)

During these talks, many suppliers complained about how GM was demanding that they reduce prices—a move that would require them to lower their costs—when, from their perspective, GM couldn't even get its own house in order. The suppliers noted that Chrysler, too, was far from perfect. Indeed, Chrysler had long been guilty of turning down or simply ignoring potentially money-saving suggestions from its suppliers—for instance, recommendations that they use a different material in a component—because the suggestions would have required running tests and making other changes in the component or in Chrysler's processes. In many cases, engineers refused even to consider such proposals, because considering them would have increased the engineers' workloads. Others were overly fearful of taking risks.

Unveiling SCORE.   It was based on these discussions with suppliers that Chrysler established SCORE as a formal program that committed the automaker to encouraging, reviewing, and acting on suppliers' ideas quickly and fairly, and to sharing the benefits of those ideas with the suppliers. The SCORE program was unveiled in 1990 at a meeting with Chrysler's top 150 suppliers. To emphasize its desire to change, Chrysler specifically asked suppliers to suggest operational changes that it could make in its own organization to reduce both its costs and those of the suppliers. Chrysler soon received a large number of written suggestions.

Chrysler's executives knew that the initiative would fail if the company simply rejected all the ideas or did not respond quickly. So in another display of strong leadership, Chrysler's top managers took personal responsibility for making sure that the company followed through on its promise to review and act on the proposals quickly. Castaing, Stallkamp, and other senior executives met once a month to review the proposals and evaluate Chrysler's responses. Initially, Chrysler's engineers wanted to reject many ideas, and senior managers had to decide when to overrule them. Determined to avoid a not-invented-here syndrome, Castaing forced through some of the ideas, pacifying the engineers by telling them to give the ideas a try simply as an experiment. Enough of the early ideas were accepted to convince suppliers that Chrysler really was open to suggestions. Soon the suggestions were pouring in, and the successes helped break down the engineers' resistance.

To get suppliers to buy into the SCORE program, Chrysler took three steps. First, it focused on what Chrysler itself was doing wrong. Second, it asked suppliers to make suggestions for changes that involved materials or parts provided by lower-tier suppliers—those that provided nonstrategic components or that supplied parts to key suppliers. Only as a third step did it turn to what the key suppliers—the ones that made strategic components or systems—were doing wrong. "The order with which we addressed these issues was important," Chrysler's Barry Price says. "The suppliers never would have gone for self-criticism before we developed a track record of correcting our own problems."

Why were suppliers willing to take the risk of expending resources to offer such ideas? The answer is that Chrysler made it profitable for them to participate in SCORE and demonstrated that it would play fair. "For many, when we fixed our operations, they made huge savings," Price says.

Perhaps even more important, Chrysler offered to share the savings generated by the suppliers' suggestions with the suppliers. Partly because it did not have the resources to audit suppliers and partly to promote trust, Chrysler initially did not quibble when it suspected that a supplier was grabbing more than half. "That first time, we didn't ask for a renegotiation," recalls Price. "We just let them know that we knew. The result: we began to get more and more ideas—sometimes even on products they didn't supply." In one case, a supplier suggested that Chrysler stop making a part out of magnesium and use plastic—an improvement that would cost the supplier the business. That suggestion saved Chrysler more than $100,000 per year.

Beyond the incentive of improving their own profitability and increasing their business with Chrysler, suppliers appreciated being listened to for a change. Under the traditional system, suppliers were rarely asked for their ideas or suggestions for improvement; they were simply given a discrete task and asked to perform that task for a price. Performance expectations were explicitly written in the contract.

Incorporating SCORE. In 1992, Chrysler made SCORE a formal part of its supplier rating system. Chrysler began to *require* suppliers to offer ideas for improvement, to maintain a vehicle system focus, and to make every effort to improve the Chrysler "extended enterprise."

Now Chrysler keeps detailed records of the number of proposals each supplier makes and the dollar savings they generate, and it uses those figures—along with the supplier's performance in the areas of price, quality, delivery, and technology—to grade the supplier's performance. In 1995, a supplier's SCORE rating was 15% of its overall rating, up from 8% in 1994—an indication of how important continual improvement throughout its value chain is to the automaker.

Chrysler has enlisted suppliers' aid in reducing vehicle weight, warranty claims, and complexity.

Since February 1994, Chrysler has given suppliers specific annual targets for savings from SCORE ideas. Although Chrysler does not penalize a supplier if it misses a SCORE target, the supplier's performance over time may eventually determine how much business it receives from the automaker. Suppliers are expected to offer suggestions that result in cost reductions equaling 5% of the supplier's sales to Chrysler. The automaker also has expanded the program to enlist suppliers' assistance in reducing vehicle weight, warranty claims, and complexity. (Suppliers receive a $20,000 credit for every part removed from a system.)

Chrysler also tracks the number of proposals awaiting a decision and the amount of time it takes to respond to a proposal. Although the job no longer falls to senior executives, Chrysler's managers continue to review engineers' evaluations of suggestions from suppliers. Managers also help suppliers with the SCORE paperwork and routinely intercede on the suppliers' behalf. In other words, the managers serve as the suppliers' advocates within the company. And to make submitting ideas even easier, SCORE is now an on-line process: a supplier can submit a proposal or check on its status at any time.

When Chrysler accepts a SCORE idea, the supplier has two choices: it can claim its half of the savings or it can share more of the savings with Chrysler in order to boost its performance rating and potentially obtain more business from the automaker.

To understand more clearly how SCORE works, consider the experience of Magna International. One of Chrysler's largest suppliers, Magna provides the automaker with seat systems, interior door and trim panels, engine and transmission systems, and a wide variety of other products. In 1993, Magna made its initial SCORE proposal, suggesting that Chrysler use a different wood-grain material on a decorative exterior molding on its minivan. The material Magna recommended cost less and offered the same quality as the material Magna had been using. Magna documented the proposal on Chrysler's supplier-buyer information form and submitted it to the responsible Chrysler buyer. The buyer then notified engineering and requested its review and consent. The entire process took approximately two weeks. Chrysler approved the proposal, which resulted in annual savings of $250,000. Since then, Magna has submitted 213 additional SCORE proposals, 129 of which Chrysler has approved—for a total cost savings of $75.5 million.

Rather than taking a share of these savings, Magna has opted to give 100% of them to Chrysler in the hopes of boosting its performance rating and winning more business. The result: since 1990, Magna's sales to Chrysler have more than doubled, from $635 million to $1.45 billion. What is more, the greater economies of scale mean that the business with Chrysler is now more profitable, says John Brice, the Magna executive director in charge of the Chrysler account.

SCORE has been astoundingly successful. In its first two years of operation, 1990 and 1991, it generated 875 ideas worth $170.8 million in annual savings to Chrysler. In 1994, suppliers submitted 3,786 ideas, which produced $504 million in annual savings. As of December 1995, Chrysler had implemented 5,300 ideas that have generated more than $1.7 billion in annual savings for the company alone. (See the exhibit "Chrysler's Profits Overtake Its Rivals'.")

ENHANCED COMMUNICATION AND COORDINATION

Chrysler promoted cooperation both among suppliers and between suppliers and Chrysler in several ways. To coordinate communication with and across suppliers more effectively, the automaker has imitated the Japanese practice of employing *resident engineers*—suppliers' engineers who work side by side with Chrysler's employees. The number of resident engineers in Chrysler's facilities has soared from fewer than 30 in 1989 to more than 300 today. Executives at suppliers and at Chrysler claim that this practice has resulted in greater trust and more reliable and timely communication of important information.

To facilitate interaction with suppliers, Chrysler has taken a number of other steps, including the creation of

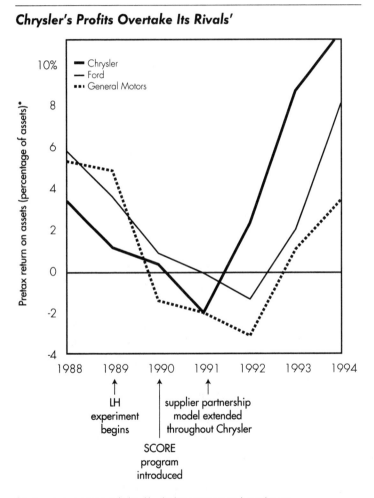

Chrysler's Profits Overtake Its Rivals'

* Pretax return on assets is calculated by dividing pretax income by total assets.
Sources: Annual reports.

a common E-mail system and the establishment of an advisory board of executives from its top 14 suppliers. In addition, it has instituted an annual meeting of its top 150 strategic suppliers and also holds quarterly meetings with each supplier to discuss strategic and performance issues and to review priorities for the coming year.

For their part, suppliers have demonstrated their trust in Chrysler by increasing their investments in dedicated assets—plant, equipment, systems, processes, and people dedicated exclusively to serving Chrysler's needs. In addition to the resident engineers, nearly all suppliers have purchased Catia (Chrysler's preferred CAD/CAM software), which at $40,000 per engineer (seat) is no small investment. (To help them obtain a lower price for Catia, Chrysler arranged a large-scale group purchase for more than 200 suppliers.)

A number of suppliers also have invested in dedicated facilities to improve their ability to make just-in-time deliveries to Chrysler and to provide it with better service. For example, Textron built a plant dedicated to producing interior trim parts for the LH and located a new design facility less than two miles from the Chrysler Technology Center. Partly as a result of investments such as those, the average distance between Chrysler's assembly plants and its suppliers' facilities has been decreasing. At Chrysler's plant in Belvidere, Illinois, where the Neon is assembled, the number of supplier shipment points has dropped by 43% and the average distance from supplier to assembler plant has shrunk by 26 miles. My previous research has demonstrated that geographic proximity lowers inventory costs and enhances communication. (See my article "Dedicated Assets: Japan's Manufacturing Edge," HBR November–December 1994.)

LONG-TERM COMMITMENTS

To earn suppliers' trust and to encourage them to invest
in dedicated assets, Chrysler is giving a growing number
of suppliers increasingly longer commitments. The average length of the contracts held by a sample of 48 of
Chrysler's suppliers on the LH program in 1994 was 4.4
years. By comparison, Chrysler's supply contracts lasted
2.1 years on average in 1989, according to a 1991 study by
Susan Helper titled "How Much Has Really Changed
between U.S. Automakers and Their Suppliers?" (*Sloan
Management Review,* Summer 1991).

Today Chrysler has given oral guarantees to more
than 90% of its suppliers that they will have the business
for the life of the model they are supplying and beyond.
Of course, the suppliers must fulfill one condition: they
must perform well on the current model and must meet
the target cost on the next. "The business is theirs to
keep forever or until they elect to lose it," Stallkamp
declares.

Suppliers make it clear that Chrysler's longer-term
commitments are having the desired effect. "I would certainly say that we are more comfortable making investments and taking risks on behalf of Chrysler than on
behalf of our other customers, with whom we have a less
secure long-term future," says Ralph Miller, CEO of auto
supplier APX International.

Surveys conducted for Ford and Chrysler in 1990,
1992, and 1993 by Planning Perspectives, an independent
market-research company, confirm that Chrysler has
made tremendous strides in developing cooperative,
trusting relationships with its suppliers. In 1990, suppliers rated Chrysler lower than both GM and Ford on five
key dimensions, including trust, responsiveness to ideas,

and efficiency. By 1993, suppliers rated Chrysler higher than Ford and GM on all five dimensions (significantly higher than GM on all five and significantly higher than Ford on three of the five).

The American Keiretsu

The American keiretsu that Chrysler has created differs from a Japanese keiretsu in two major respects. First, Japanese manufacturers like Toyota and Nissan typically own 20% to 50% of the equity of their largest suppliers; Chrysler does not and could not take similar stakes. Toyota, for example, has only about 310 suppliers, and those with which it has equity ties, about 50, typically depend on it for two-thirds of their sales. So their destinies are closely intertwined. By comparison, Chrysler still has a much larger group of suppliers, and few of its most important suppliers depend on it for a majority of their sales. Second, approximately 20% of the executives at Toyota's and Nissan's major supplier companies formerly worked for those automakers. This intimacy leads to a high level of understanding and a common culture that Chrysler could never duplicate.

However, Chrysler's arrangement has its advantages. It is much easier for Chrysler to drop underperforming suppliers than it is for Toyota or Nissan. Because those companies cannot drop suppliers so easily, they are under greater pressure to commit resources to help suppliers improve. This assistance almost certainly benefits rivals—including Chrysler—that buy from those suppliers.

Chrysler's formal programs that measure results and offer incentives for improvement ideas are probably more suitable for the U.S. business environment than the

Japanese companies' relatively informal approach would be. One could argue that without formal programs such as SCORE, suppliers would not devote the same resources to generating ideas. As Stallkamp observes, "SCORE is a success because it is a communications program, not just a cost-cutting program. By learning how to communicate, we've learned how to help each other." The level of communication needed to make a supplier partnership productive simply may not happen naturally in the U.S. business environment.

On the other hand, Chrysler's policies for building partnerships seem to be too successful in one sense: they appear to be making it harder for the company to continue to shrink its supplier base, which it would like to do to reduce coordination costs, improve quality, achieve even greater economies of scale, and, last but not least, strengthen its ties with the suppliers it retains. The shrinkage rate has slowed. Chrysler still has almost four times as many suppliers in the United States as Toyota does in Japan.

In addition, Chrysler still lags far behind its Japanese competitors in converting lower levels of its supply chain to the new supplier-management approach. Its biggest suppliers are only beginning to replicate programs such as presourcing, target costing, and SCORE in their own supply chains.

Even if Chrysler has a long way to go, the progress it has made in the last seven years is nonetheless remarkable. Its success to date in building an American keiretsu—or, as its leaders prefer to call it, Chrysler's "extended enterprise"—proves that decades of adversarial relations can be overcome. As Steve Zimmer, Chrysler's director of operations and strategy for procurement and supply, notes, "We've learned that you don't have to be Japanese to have a keiretsu-like relationship with suppliers." Chrysler has proved that highly productive partnerships with suppliers not only can flourish in the United States but are the wave of the future.

How Supplier Partnerships Helped Revive Chrysler

PARTNERSHIPS WITH SUPPLIERS have helped Chrysler improve performance significantly by speeding up product development, lowering development costs, and reducing procurement costs, thereby contributing to increases in Chrysler's market share and profitability.

Shortening the Product Development Cycle

Company documents indicate that Chrysler has reduced the amount of time it takes to develop a new vehicle from 234 weeks (the average product-development cycle for new-vehicle programs in the 1980s) to 183 weeks for the LH program. The next version of the LH—scheduled for introduction in late 1997—is on schedule to reach the target of 160 weeks from concept approval to volume production. Thus, since 1989, Chrysler has reduced the time it takes to develop a new vehicle by more than 40%. Also, Chrysler's productivity increased during the 1980s: whereas the automaker developed only four new vehicles between 1980 and 1989, it has already developed and introduced six new vehicles since 1990, without increasing the size of its total engineering staff.

Partnerships with suppliers have been essential to speeding product development. Under its old system, Chrysler devoted 12 to 18 months of the development process to sending out bids for quotations, analyzing bids, rebidding, negotiating contracts, and bringing suppliers on board and up to speed. After selecting suppliers, Chrysler would have to spend additional time responding to problems they encountered when trying to manufacture a part they usually had not designed. Often suppliers did not even know they had won the business until 75 to 100 weeks before volume production. Under the new system, suppliers become involved at the conceptual stage (about 180 weeks before volume production on the LH, Neon, and Cirrus/Stratus programs), giving them an extra 18 to 24 months to prepare for volume production and additional time to work out potential problems early in the process.

Reducing the Overall Costs of the Vehicle Program

The cost of developing and launching a new model can be divided into four categories: engineering, research, and development (ER&D), which consists of the costs associated with designing and engineering a new vehicle; tools, such as dies and molds; facilities, such as new conveyors, presses, and welding lines in the plant; and preproduction and launch (PP&L) expenses, such as training and manufacturing preparation. For a typical Chrysler program, roughly 15% to 20% of total costs are in ER&D, 40% to 45% are in tools, 25% to 30% are in facilities, and 5% to 10% are in PP&L. Since 1989, Chrysler has been able to reduce overall program costs significantly. Before Chrysler adopted Japanese-style supplier partnerships, its investments in preproduction plants, equipment, and training, and its piece costs during production often ran 25% to 50% over budget.

By involving suppliers early in product development and giving them greater responsibility for design and manufacturing, Chrysler has sped up the product development process—and has needed fewer engineering hours per vehicle. For instance, ER&D costs for the LH program were roughly $300 million (or 20% of the LH's $1.6 billion program). By reducing ER&D time by 24% over previous programs, Chrysler saved approximately $75 million in developing the LH. The company's 1998 LH model will save an additional 15% in ER&D over the 1993 model.

Faster development cycles also have helped to reduce program costs because hard tools can be purchased closer to volume production. Chrysler now purchases hard tools approximately 50 to 60 weeks before volume production, as opposed to 75 to 100 weeks before, as it did when product development was slower. Thus the company saves up to 12 months of investment in hard tools. Given that 40% to 45% of program costs are in tools, Chrysler saved approximately $60 million on the LH program by delaying the purchase of hard tools (assuming a conservative 10% cost of capital).

Chrysler also has saved money by reducing the number of changes in hard tools after they have been cut. Historically, the lengthy development process did not produce the first prototype until about 65 weeks before volume production. However, the lead time on many hard tools was more than 65 weeks, so work on hard tools had to begin before the first prototype was completed. When problems were discovered in the prototype, Chrysler had to ask for corrections to hard tools that already had been ordered. With the LH program, Chrysler involved suppliers earlier on; as a result, the first prototype was completed 24 weeks earlier than in previous programs—and hard tools were cut *after* Chrysler and its suppliers identified problems with the prototype.

Also, because Chrysler now has suppliers take responsibility for both the prototype and the volume production, it has been able to reduce time, communication problems, and incompatibility in the parts. In fact, the overall cost to develop a new vehicle seems to be gradually declining at Chrysler. The LH program cost $1.6 billion, the Dodge Ram truck cost $1.3 billion, the Neon cost $1.2 billion, and the Cirrus/Stratus cost less than $1 billion. These costs compare favorably with the development costs of similar models developed by GM and Ford. For instance, the Neon is similar to GM's Saturn ($3.5 billion to develop) and Ford's Escort ($2.5 billion). The Cirrus/Stratus is similar to Ford's Mondeo/Contour, which cost $6 billion to develop, according to the *Economist* (April 23, 1994).

Reducing Procurement (Transaction) Costs

Since 1988, Chrysler has reduced its number of buyers by 30% and has sharply increased the dollar value of goods procured by each buyer. Those results were made possible by reducing the number of overall suppliers (reducing search costs) and eliminating the competitive bidding system (reducing negotiation and contracting costs). In a presentation to suppliers in November 1994, purchasing chief Thomas Stallkamp requested that suppliers eliminate sales representatives altogether and shift those resources to engineering.

Increasing Market Share and Profitability

Because unit sales of vehicles increase substantially in both the United States and Japan after a major model change, automakers that develop new models more quickly than competitors can increase their market share. Chrysler's ability to produce more new models has contributed to its increased share of the U.S. car and truck market—14.7% in 1994, up from 12.2% in 1987. This is Chrysler's highest share in the U.S. market in 25 years. Chrysler also has dramatically improved its profitability. Its return on assets, which throughout the 1980s tended to be lower than its competitors', has been the highest among U.S. automakers since 1992. Its profit per vehicle has increased from approximately $250 in the 1980s (taking the average from 1985 through 1989) to $2,110 in 1994.

Originally published in July–August 1996
Reprint 96403

The author would like to thank the Reginald H. Jones Center for Management Policy, Strategy, and Organization at the Wharton School and Michigan Future for their support of this research. He would also like to thank Thomas Stallkamp and the many others at Chrysler who assisted him.

The Power of Trust in Manufacturer-Retailer Relationships

NIRMALYA KUMAR

Executive Summary

MANUFACTURERS AND RETAILERS traditionally have seen each other as adversaries, but the benefits generated by trusting relationships between such old foes as Procter & Gamble Company and Wal-Mart Stores show that fear and intimidation may not be the most effective way for manufacturers and retailers to deal with each other after all. Studies of manufacturer-retailer relationships in a variety of industries reveal that exploiting power has three major drawbacks: it can come back to haunt a company if the balance of power changes; victims will ultimately seek ways to resist such exploitation; and working as partners allows retailers and manufacturers to provide customers with greater value than they can when they try to exploit each other.

To build a trusting relationship with their weaker partners, powerful companies can build systems that strive both to compensate their partners fairly for their contributions and to resolve differences in a manner that their partners perceive as fair. These systems ensure that there is two-way communication, that all channel partners are dealt with equitably, and that partners can appeal channel policies and decisions. In addition, they provide partners with a coherent rationale for policies and ensure that partners are treated with respect.

Moving a relationship from the power game to the trust game is difficult, requiring a change in culture, management systems, and attitudes. But the success of organizations such as Marks & Spencer, Kraft, and E.J. Ekornes all testify to the benefits of making the effort. In rapidly changing environments, success will go to those who learn to make the leap of faith.

IN INDUSTRIES AS DIVERSE AS pharmaceuticals, consumer packaged goods, hardware, apparel, and furniture, the balance of power between manufacturers and retailers is shifting. Thanks to the rise of specialty superstores, the formation of buying alliances, and a consolidating wave of mergers and acquisitions, a relative handful of retailers often now control access to enormous numbers of consumers. Manufacturers that had dominated their retailers are now finding that megaretailers hold the upper hand. In Europe, for example, the sales of each of the top six food retailers exceed the individual sales of all food manufacturers, with the exception of Nestlé and Unilever. And in the United States, Wal-Mart Stores' revenues are three times those of Procter & Gamble Company. (See the table "Three Forces Fuel Rising Retailer Power.")

This shift raises some important questions. Although powerful companies can, and often do, use their strength to wring concessions from their vulnerable counterparts, is the use of fear or intimidation the most effective way to manage such relationships? Or does trust produce greater benefits? And if trust is more beneficial to both sides, what policies and procedures help breed it?

With the help of colleagues at U.S. and European universities, I have been developing a research database since 1988 to answer those questions. Almost 3,000 U.S.

Three Forces Fuel Rising Retailer Power

Emergence of Megaformats	**Mergers and Acquisitions**	**Horizontal Alliances**
Megaretailing formats include:	Previously independent department-store chains now belong to retailing conglomerates.	Some European retailers have organized themselves into cross-border buying alliances to bargain more effectively with manufacturers.
Category killers Border Book Shops, Circuit City Stores, Home Depot, Office Depot, Staples, Toys "R" Us	***Federated Department Stores*** Macy's, Bloomingdale's, Stern's, Rich's, Goldsmith's, Lazarus, Burdines, the Bon Marché	***European Retail Alliance*** Royal Ahold (Netherlands) Argyll Group (United Kingdom) Casino-Guichard Perrachon & CIE (France)
Warehouse clubs Price Club, Costco Wholesale Club, Sam's Wholesale Club	***May Department Stores Company*** Lord & Taylor, Foley's, Robinsons-May, Hecht's, Kaufmann's, Filene's, Famous Barr, Meier & Frank	***Eurogroup*** BML (Austria) Coop Switzerland Rewe-Handelsgruppe (Germany) Vendex International (Netherlands)
Discount supercenters Super Kmart Centers, Wal-Mart Supercenters	Similar conglomerates have also emerged outside the United States: Coles Meyer (Australia) Metro (Germany) Royal Ahold (Netherlands) Ito-Yokado Company (Japan)	

and European executives have responded to our surveys and reported on more than 1,500 manufacturer-retailer relationships. In addition, I have consulted and con-ducted interviews with several major retailers and manu-facturers in the United States, Latin America, Asia, and Europe. Through our efforts, my colleagues and I have collected informa-tion on manufacturer-retailer relationships in such industries as auto-mobiles, computers, consumer packaged goods, earth-moving equipment, replacement tires, semiconductors, telecommunications, and vehicle leasing.

Exploiting power may work in the short run, but it is self-defeating in the long run.

We found that although exploiting power may be advantageous in the short run, it tends to be self-defeating in the long run for three main reasons:

Exploiting power to extract unfair concessions can come back to haunt a company if its position of power changes. When they had the upper hand, consumer packaged-goods manufacturers such as Procter & Gamble used to limit the quantities of high-demand products they would deliver to a given supermarket chain, insist that the supermarket carry all sizes of a cer-tain product, and demand that the supermarket partici-pate in promotional programs. Now it's payback time. In the past ten years, supermarket chains have become enormous and manufacturers' battles for shelf space have intensified. As a result, the chains have been able to demand that manufacturers pay them for carrying new products and to force them to participate in the chains' promotional programs.

When companies systematically exploit their advantage, their victims ultimately seek ways to resist. Retailers may form associations or buying groups, develop private labels, or pursue vertical integration or mergers to counteract the power of manufacturers. European retailers such as Carrefour, Casino, J. Sainsbury, and Migros have developed quality private-label brands to compete with internationally renowned manufacturer brands. And one major reason for the recent merger and acquisition activity in the U.S. drugstore industry is the desire of drugstore chains to increase their purchasing clout with pharmaceutical companies.

For their part, many manufacturers are reacting to the pressure tactics of traditional retailers by seeking direct links to end users through the Internet and mail-order operations and by creating their own stores. Apparel and accessory designers such as Donna Karan, Giorgio Armani, and Liz Claiborne have been opening factory outlets and their own downtown stores, and Nike and Sony Corporation have established megastores in cities such as Chicago, London, and Tokyo. Airlines are beginning to let consumers book reservations over the Internet, bypassing travel agents. And many consumer-products manufacturers have created sites on the World Wide Web, hoping this link to consumers will ultimately permit them to reduce or eliminate their dependence on retailers and dealers.

In service industries such as entertainment, one can see a similar "manufacturer" backlash. Such major producers of television programs as Warner Brothers and Paramount Pictures Corporation are spending huge sums on their new TV networks to compete with ABC,

NBC, CBS, and Fox. The traditional networks brought this development on themselves by using their monopolistic power coercively in the past.

By working together as partners, retailers and manufacturers can provide the greatest value to customers at the lowest possible cost.   Take the supermarket industry, in which adversarial relationships still prevail. Industry experts believe that seamless partnerships between manufacturers and supermarkets would accelerate the deployment of sophisticated systems such as just-in-time delivery, electronic data interchange, and so-called efficient-consumer-response systems that permit manufacturers to monitor sales in stores and to produce and ship their goods in response to actual consumer demand. Such cooperative systems could squeeze $30 billion in excess costs out of the industry by eliminating superfluous inventory, duplicate functions, and various middlemen. Moreover, the results witnessed when manufacturers and supermarket chains do cooperate suggest that both sides could increase sales volume by working together to customize offerings at different stores and for different end users. Cooperation between Kraft Foods and supermarket chains such as Publix Super Markets in Florida and Wegmans Food Markets in upstate New York has generated significant returns for both sides.

The Nature of Trust

Initially in my research, I was surprised by how often manufacturers and retailers mentioned trust when discussing their relationships. What did they mean when they said they trusted someone?

The immediate response of most managers was that trust involved *dependability*—that they believed that their partners were reliable and would honor their word. The marketing director of a multinational manufacturer of consumer packaged goods observed that the retailers that his company tended to trust fulfilled agreements without always coming back to demand additional concessions or to request greater support. And if the retailers requested promotional funds in exchange for preferred shelf positions, then the manufacturer would find its products in those positions on subsequent visits to the retailers' stores.

Of course, honesty and dependability do not always promote trust. A partner that frequently promises to punish you and always follows through is honest and dependable but is not a company in which you place your trust. What really distinguishes trusting from distrusting relationships is the ability of the parties to make a *leap of faith:* they believe that each is interested in the other's welfare and that neither will act without first considering the action's impact on the other.

Because of shifts in competitive dynamics in recent years, many companies are growing increasingly concerned about the level of faith that their distribution channel partners have in them. One study that I conducted with Lisa Scheer of the University of Missouri at Columbia and Jan-Benedict Steenkamp of the Catholic University of Leuven in Belgium measured the extent to which automobile retailers in the United States believed that the manufacturer whose product line they carried would honor its commitments (dependability) and consider the best interests of the retailer (faith). The manufacturers included U.S., European, and Japanese companies. The results demonstrated that Ford Motor

Company generated greater trust among its dealers than General Motors Corporation or Chrysler Corporation did. However, the Japanese manufacturers earned a higher level of trust than any of the U.S. or European companies. The executives of the U.S. automobile manufacturer that commissioned the study were concerned about the lack of faith that their dealers had in them because they believed that the support and service that dealers provided to end users would become increasingly important in attracting and retaining customers.

During my field research, I observed that manufacturers and retailers tend to believe that the partners they trust also trust them. However, an analysis of the database demonstrated that such an assumption is not always warranted. In a study I conducted with Jonathan Hibbard of Boston University and Louis Stern of Northwestern University, we examined the relationships between a major manufacturer of replacement automobile parts and 429 of its retailers. It turned out that the manufacturer had a high level of trust (an average of 5.8 on a 7-point scale) in 218 of the retailers that distrusted the manufacturer (an average of 2.6 on the same 7-point scale).[1] A further investigation revealed the pitfall of this blind trust: Many of those 218 retailers were actively seeking and developing alternative sources of supply, whereas the manufacturer, which assumed that its trust in the retailers was mutual, was not exploring alternatives to those retailers.

The Benefits and Limits of Trust

A crucial question is whether powerful manufacturers or retailers receive more tangible benefits from building trusting relationships with partners than from exploiting their clout. Is trust more than just a feel-good phenomenon? The results of the study that I just described certainly suggest that it is: the retailers that trusted the manufacturer were 12% more committed to the relationship (as measured by their intent to carry the manufacturer's products in the future), were 22% less likely to have developed alternative sources of supply, and performed at higher levels for the manufacturer than the retailers that did not trust it. (See the exhibit "Having Trusting Retailers Pays Off.")

I used two different metrics to evaluate the retailers' performance for the manufacturer. One was the sales generated for the manufacturer and the second was a more holistic but more subjective evaluation. (See "A Scale to Assess Retailer Performance" at the end of this article.) The results showed that retailers with a high level of trust in the manufacturer generated 78% more sales than those with a low level. The results using the holistic evaluation were less dramatic. Still, retailers that reported that they trusted the manufacturer highly were rated as performing 11% better, a percentage that is statistically significant. When my colleagues and I used the two metrics in other industries, including vehicle leasing and computer peripherals, the results were similar.

Trust brings other benefits as well. It creates a reservoir of goodwill that helps preserve the relationship when, as will inevitably happen, one party engages in an act that its partner considers destructive. The growth of multiple-channel distribution systems has made such situations much more common in recent years. For example, manufacturers such as Compaq Computer Corporation and Goodyear Tire and Rubber Company are aggressively wooing faster-growing distributors, including so-called category killers such as Circuit City Stores

Having Trusting Retailers Pays Off

The four comparisons below show how a manufacturer of replacement automotive parts reaped greater benefits when its retailers had a high level of trust in it. Each of the manufacturer's 429 retailers was classified into one of two groups—retailers with high trust in the manufacturer or retailers with low trust in the manufacturer—based on the retailer's response to our scale measuring retailer trust. Then the two groups of high- and low-trust retailers were compared on the extent to which they were developing alternative sources of supply; their intention to continue carrying the manufacturer's product line; unit sales generated for the manufacturer; and the manufacturer's rating of the retailers' performance, measured using the scale that we developed for that purpose. (See "A Scale to Assess Retailer Performance" at the end of this article.) The average scores for each group were converted so that the low-trust retailers' average score equaled 100 and the high-trust retailers' average score was proportionally scaled.

Retailers' Development of Alternative Sources of Supply

low trust (100)   high trust (78)

Retailers' Commitment to the Manufacturer

low trust (100)   high trust (112)

Retailers' Sales of the Manufacturer's Product Line

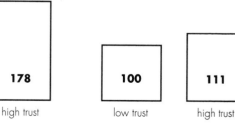

low trust (100)   high trust (178)

Retailers' Performance as Rated by the Manufacturer

low trust (100)   high trust (111)

and mass merchandisers such as Sears, Roebuck and Company and Wal-Mart. These moves are infuriating their traditional independent dealers, who resent the better price and delivery terms that their rivals are receiving. Our research shows that in such situations, trusting retailers tend to be understanding and blame competitive conditions, whereas distrustful retailers tend to hold the manufacturer personally responsible. Consequently, trusting retailers are less likely to retaliate by dropping or neglecting the manufacturer's product line than distrustful retailers are.

Trust helps manufacturer-retailer relationships realize their full potential. When both sides trust each other, they are able to share confidential information, to invest in understanding each other's business, and to customize their information systems or dedicate people and resources to serve each other better. A trusting party typically will not feel it needs to monitor its counterpart's behavior; thus it can cut its monitoring costs. Last

When both sides trust each other, they can share information and invest in understanding each other's business.

but not least, trust allows a company to capture the hearts and minds of channel partners so that they will go the extra mile. The relationship between Procter & Gamble and Wal-Mart illustrates how even powerful adversaries can benefit from deciding to base their relationships on trust. (See "Two Tough Companies Learn to Dance Together" at the end of this article.)

Can a company have its cake and eat it, too? Can a company build trust while seeking to retain or increase its leverage or power over a partner? My research suggests not. Rather, trust requires companies to relinquish some of their independence, or, to put it another way, to become more dependent on each other.

In one study, Scheer, Steenkamp, and I separated more than 400 manufacturer-retailer relationships into four categories of differing levels of interdependence. On average, a company's level of trust and its satisfaction with the relationship (as measured on the 1-to-7 scale) were the highest and the level of perceived conflict was lowest in the relationships in which there was a high level of interdependence. (See the exhibit "Effects of Interdependence.")

If one thinks about it, this finding is logical. Effective relationships require both parties to make contributions. A hostage company often will try to reduce its depen-

---

Effects of Interdependence

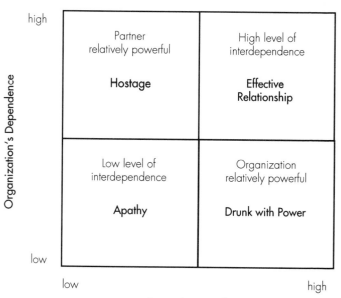

high

Organization's Dependence

Partner relatively powerful **Hostage**	High level of interdependence **Effective Relationship**
Low level of interdependence **Apathy**	Organization relatively powerful **Drunk with Power**

low

low   high

Partner's Dependence

dence on its partner, an effort that only moves the relationship into the apathy quadrant. A hostage would gain much more by becoming a more valuable resource to the partner, thereby moving the relationship toward the high interdependence quadrant. Although people in many societies are socialized to prize independence, self-sufficiency, and unilateral control, no company is an island. Effective companies build networks based on interdependence.

Although I advocate relationships based on trust, I recognize that there are underlying tensions in any manufacturer-retailer relationship. The trust strategy works only with those partners that are willing to play the trust game. Furthermore, regardless of how deeply two partners trust each other, there will always be areas of difference because the two parties inevitably will have some goals that are different.

The limits of trust are especially obvious when the manufacturer and the retailer do not have a mutually exclusive relationship. It is easier to develop trust when manufacturers offer territorial exclusivity and when retailers do not carry product lines of competing manufacturers. But if a product needs to be distributed widely, as most consumer packaged goods do, or if a retailer needs to carry a wide variety of brands, as supermarkets and mass merchandisers do, then such exclusivity is impossible.

Operating in numerous relationships with different practices is a challenge for the best of companies. They may be tempted to apply what they have learned in one relationship to other relationships. Procter & Gamble, for example, has tried to use two pillars of its successful dealings with Wal-Mart to support its relationships with other retailers. The pillars are multifunctional customer teams—each of which focuses on a single customer—and everyday low pricing (lower standard prices and an end to special promotions). P&G discovered, however, that some retailers were not large enough to warrant such teams—or even a full-time person. And some retailers have retaliated against P&G's everyday low pricing policy by reducing shelf space for P&G products.

Finally, trust is rarely all-encompassing. One may trust the partner on some issues but not on others, just as I trust my neighbor to take care of my plants but not my car while I am on vacation. Employees who interact with their company's partners must understand which information, skills, and technologies are to be protected and which are to be shared. Partners have to understand that the information they receive is to be treated in confidence. McDonald's Corporation's contract with its franchisees gives McDonald's the right to take over a franchisee's operations if the latter discloses confidential information. However, such concerns must not be allowed to impede the sharing of the information and skills required for the relationship to flourish.

> *Trust is rarely all-encompassing. One may trust the partner on some issues but not on others.*

Creating Trust

Of course, the vast majority of manufacturer-retailer relationships are unbalanced. Huge manufacturers such as Mercedes-Benz sell their products through small mom-and-pop dealers; and major retailers such as France's Carrefour, Japan's Ito-Yokado, Britain's Marks & Spencer, and America's Toys "R" Us buy from numerous relatively small manufacturers. In a relationship of unequals, how can the powerful party build a trusting relationship? The key is to treat the weaker, vulnerable partner fairly. Fairness encompasses two types of justice: *distributive justice,* or the perceived fairness of the outcomes received, and *procedural justice,* or the perceived fairness of the powerful party's process for managing the relationship.

DISTRIBUTIVE JUSTICE

This type of justice deals with how the pie is shared, or how the benefits and burdens are divided between partners. Although some companies use their power to maximize their own benefits, others realize they have some responsibility for their partner's profitability. An outstanding example is Marks & Spencer, the British retailer. One of its guiding principles is to work closely with suppliers in long-term partnerships.

Marks & Spencer believes that manufacturers, especially those in the Far East, are often so keen to get its business that they will accept prices that are too low to warrant the investments necessary for improving their operations and products further. Because Marks & Spencer seeks long-term relationships with suppliers, it views that situation as unacceptable—as one that hurts both sides.

When its relationship with an existing supplier becomes inequitable, Marks & Spencer's managers strive to restore the balance. The story of a kitchen product that Marks & Spencer had developed jointly with a manufacturer is a case in point. Four months after the product's introduction in 1995, the manufacturer realized that it had miscalculated the amount of labor required to make the product and, as a result, had underpriced the product and was losing money on the deal. Because of the miscalculation, however, the product provided outstanding value for Marks & Spencer's customers and was a big hit.

When the manufacturer brought the problem to the attention of Marks & Spencer's managers, the managers explained that they could not change the retail price because it was already listed in their catalogue. Instead, Marks & Spencer helped the manufacturer to reengineer the product. By cutting a few labor-intensive steps and reducing packaging, the two companies were able to lower the manufacturer's costs without jeopardizing the product's performance. In addition, Marks & Spencer cut its own gross margin on the product and gave that money to the manufacturer.

Although highly unusual, Marks & Spencer is not unique. Another organization that understands the long-term importance of allowing channel partners to earn a fair return is Toyota Motor Corporation's Lexus division. When Lexus established itself in the United States in the 1980s, it decided it wanted its dealers to be able to invest in the facilities, systems, and personnel required to deliver extraordinary customer service. As a consequence, Lexus makes it possible for dealers to make several thousand dollars on the sale of each new car—considerably above the industry average.

PROCEDURAL JUSTICE

Research on justice in a variety of settings indicates that due process, or the fairness of a party's procedures and policies for dealing with its vulnerable partners, has stronger effects on relationships than distributive justice does. Managers find this idea rather counterintuitive. In one instance, my colleagues and I were working with executives of a major automobile manufacturer that wanted to enhance the level of trust that its dealers had in it. The executives were skeptical that dealers cared about anything other than margins or outcomes and decided to raise the margins they offered to their dealers. But they also were willing to support a study of how the two types of justice affect trust.

This study of 800 automobile dealers in the United States and the Netherlands supported the contention that although both distributive and procedural justice enhance trust, the latter is considerably more important. The outcomes from a relationship are affected by many factors (including competitive conditions), only some of which are under the control of the more powerful partner. However, the more powerful partner is always considered in control of its policies and procedures. The weaker partner, therefore, sees the powerful partner's system of procedural justice as reflecting more accurately the latter's real attitudes toward the former. Systems that are procedurally just are built on the following six principles:

Bilateral Communication.   The more powerful party is willing to engage in two-way communication with its partners. Marks & Spencer views an open and honest dialogue as a sign of a healthy relationship and encourages its suppliers to be proactive and frank in pointing out the company's weaknesses. It has a number of procedures in place to encourage such communication. The CEO of Marks & Spencer meets his counterparts in suppliers' organizations periodically. Regular suppliers are given a keycard to enter Marks & Spencer's head offices, enabling them to drop by at any time to discuss issues. Although most make appointments first, having the card makes them feel that they are members of the Marks & Spencer family. In addition, Marks & Spencer organizes joint trips with its suppliers to trade shows and to visit foreign suppliers of raw materials. The trips enhance mutual understanding and help both parties identify new products that they could develop together.

Other companies have different practices to solicit input from partners. At Anheuser-Busch Companies, the chairman makes it a rule to meet with a 15-member panel of wholesalers four times a year in order to hear their suggestions and complaints. Oldsmobile allowed its car dealers to sit on a committee to review its advertising contract with Leo Burnett Company.

Impartiality. The more powerful party deals with channel partners equitably. Although it is impossible to treat all channel partners identically, it is important to give partners equitable opportunities. When Marks & Spencer has multiple manufacturers supplying a single product category, it attempts to ensure that everyone gets a fair share of the business. It also tries to minimize major changes in the volume of business awarded to suppliers from one year to the next. Any major shifts take place only over a period of years, so that suppliers have time to adjust their production capacities and do not feel unfairly treated.

Some powerful manufacturers, including Kraft, have started to create flexible programs or service menus that allow even the smallest retailers to participate in promotional programs. Such innovations, which allow for customization within established boundaries, are necessary because retailers operate under different conditions and strategies. Kraft sets up individual funds to help retailers develop their joint merchandising programs. A retailer may use the money to feature Kraft products in its own store circulars, to advertise on local television, or to offer discount coupons. And different retailers may use their funds to feature different Kraft products. Kraft and the retailer make the spending decision together, relying heavily on market-research data.

Impartiality is a very sensitive issue for many dealers. In the U.S. publishing and pharmaceutical industries, there have been numerous lawsuits over this issue during the past few years. Many book retailers and independent pharmacies complain that manufacturers do not use the same pricing and promotion schedules for all retailers.

Refutability. The smaller or more vulnerable partners can appeal the more powerful party's channel policies and decisions. Manufacturers such as Caterpillar, DuPont, and 3M have dealer advisory councils at which dealers can air their concerns. Marks & Spencer has a rule that a supplier always can appeal a decision to a higher level in the company. The way in which a recent potentially divisive disagreement between a Marks & Spencer buyer and an upholstery manufacturer was resolved provides a good example. The buyer thought that allowing customers to take home small fabric swatches would make it easier for them to make a selection. Accordingly, the buyer asked the manufacturer to provide more swatches. Initially, the manufacturer did not mind. But so many customers wanted the swatches that giving them away became a considerable cost. The manufacturer tried to convince the buyer that it should be reimbursed until it was proved that the program would generate sufficient additional sales to justify the extra cost. When the buyer refused, the manufacturer contacted the head of the division, who invited the manufacturer to meet with him and asked the buyer to attend. At the meeting, the division head appeased the manufacturer, assuring it that Marks & Spencer would compensate it if the program did not soon produce enough sales to cover the additional costs.

Explanation. The more powerful party provides its partners with a coherent rationale for its channel decisions and policies. Although those in power often feel that they have the right to make decisions without explaining them, that attitude has a detrimental impact on trust. For this reason, Marks & Spencer takes pains to explain its policies and actions to its suppliers. At an annual meeting attended by its 300 store managers and its major suppliers, members of Marks & Spencer's board of directors explain their vision and strategies. In addition, Marks & Spencer's personnel go with individual manufacturers to Marks & Spencer stores to help explain how the retailer is presenting and selling the manufacturer's merchandise. Decisions and policies are more likely to be accepted by partners when the logic behind them is apparent.

Familiarity. The powerful party understands or is aware of the local conditions under which its channel partners operate. Before Marks & Spencer enters into a relationship with a new manufacturer, it will make a number of visits to the manufacturer's plants and will host meetings between its buyers, merchandisers, and designers and their counterparts in the manufacturer's organization. Marks & Spencer believes that this interaction is critical because it permits the retailer to ascertain the ability of the manufacturer to meet its requests or demands. Similarly, Square D Company, a U.S. manufacturer of electrical and electronic products, encourages its salespeople to call on the dealers' customers jointly with its dealers' salespeople. Other companies purposely recruit personnel from customers and suppliers to work in the jobs in which understanding those customers or suppliers is essential.

Courtesy. Treating a partner with respect is crucial for building the interpersonal chemistry that is the foundation of most successful manufacturer-retailer relationships. Ultimately, relationships between companies are actually relationships between teams of people on either side. As companies recognize this fact, they are changing the way they assign personnel to various accounts. Some companies assign employees to accounts based on the match between employees' personalities and the culture of the customer or supplier. Sherwin-Williams Company, the paint manufacturer, lets managers from Sears, Roebuck and Company help select the Sherwin-Williams people who will handle the Sears account.

Opportunities for attractive returns are usually the magnet for a relationship, but procedural fairness is the glue that holds the relationship together. It is expensive and risky to try to retain partners by giving them higher margins than competitors give them. In contrast, developing procedurally just systems requires greater effort, energy, investment, patience, and perhaps even a change in organizational culture. But for precisely those reasons, developing such systems is more likely to lead to sustainable competitive advantage.

Moving from the Power Game to the Trust Game

Many companies that want to move from conventional adversarial relationships to channel partnerships based on trust find that they do not yet possess the capabilities necessary to make the transition. It is not enough for powerful manufacturers or retailers just to start calling their channel counterparts partners. The culture, people, management systems, and attitude that the trust game requires are fundamentally different from those used in the power game. (See the exhibit "Power and Trust.") Past practices have to be unlearned before the new approach to managing relationships can be adopted. (See "How Ekornes Turned Its Retailers into Partners" at the end of this article.)

Companies that want to develop trust pay greater attention to partner selection. They select partners that bring distinctive competencies but similar values. As who the partner is becomes more important, traditional methods of selecting partners become less appropriate. When J.E. Ekornes, the Norwegian furniture manufacturer, decided to move from a traditional power relationship with its retailers to partnerships based on trust, it "fired" those retailers that did not share its values in their strategies, their views of their roles, and their views on how to treat customers. It reduced its number of retailers in France by a third and in Sweden by half.

For relationships to bloom and achieve their full potential, they must be flexible and informal. Long, detailed contracts are inconsistent with building relationships based on trust and simply get in the way. Companies that base their relationships on trust either have minimal contracts or do away with contracts altogether.

A majority of wholesalers in Japan operate without contracts. Caterpillar dealership agreements can be terminated without cause by either party with 90 days' notice. What holds these relationships together is not legal force but mutual obligations and opportunities. Marks & Spencer regards its relationships with its suppliers as morally binding and does not have legal contracts. Yet

Power and Trust

	The Power Game	The Trust Game
Modus operandi:	Create fear	Create trust
Guiding principle:	Pursue self-interest	Pursue what's fair
Negotiating strategy:	Avoid dependence by playing multiple partners off against each other	Create interdependence by limiting the number of partnerships
	Retain flexibility for self but lock in partners by raising their switching costs	Both parties signal commitment through specialized investments, which lock them in
Communication:	Primarily unilateral	Bilateral
Influence:	Through coercion	Through expertise
Contracts:	"Closed," or formal, detailed, and short-term	"Open," or informal and long-term
	Use competitive bidding frequently	Check market prices occasionally
Conflict management:	Reduce conflict potential through detailed contracts	Reduce conflict potential by selecting partners with similar values and by increasing mutual understanding
	Resolve conflict through the legal system	Resolve conflicts through procedures such as mediation or arbitration

there is almost no turnover in its suppliers and some of its relationships are more than 100 years old.

Companies should encourage employees assigned to an account to learn the partner's business and to work together with the partner to discover opportunities that will benefit both. Companies often find that they have to reorganize to achieve this type of focus or orientation. Kraft, for example, did away with its disparate sales forces for Kraft, General Foods, and Oscar Mayer Foods Corporation and assigned its people to 200 cross-functional business teams, each of which is dedicated to a single major retail customer. Those teams—whose members include category managers and information specialists as well as marketing, operations, and finance and accounting personnel—work much more intimately with partners than the sales forces did.

Often, the teams function as consultants to the retail partners. In one instance, a Kraft team conducted a six-month study of a retailer's dairy case. The team made recommendations on how to reorganize the shelf space and suggested new items that the retailer could add to take advantage of consumer trends. As a result, the retailer enjoyed a 22% gain in volume and suffered fewer stock-outs. Kraft benefited from the improved positioning of its high-demand products: its sales to the account increased by a similar magnitude.[2]

Companies that play the power game often prefer their employees not to develop personal relationships with their counterparts at channel partners, fearing such ties will weaken employees' resolve to push hard for the best possible deal. To prevent that from happening, Jose Ignacio Lopez, GM's former purchasing czar, reassigned buyers to suppliers with whom they had not dealt. He found that procurement prices declined. In contrast, companies that play the trust game encourage personal ties with their channel partners. Because they know that it takes a long time to build and maintain a relationship based on trust, many of these companies attempt to minimize employee turnover. Of course, some employee turnover is inevitable. One advantage of dedicating a cross-functional team to an account is that the relationship is less dependent on any one employee.

The trust game also has implications for the type of people that a company recruits to work with channel partners and how those people are managed. Traditional manufacturers' salespeople and retail buyers have had a volume or price focus. They need to be replaced by *relationship managers* with appropriate bedside manners. Incentive and performance measurement programs often have to be changed as well. For example, P&G used to reward its U.S. sales managers for transferring inventory from its production site to the retailer's warehouse or stockroom, regardless of what was best for the retailer. Now P&G rewards them for maximizing the profits of both P&G and its retailers. And Wal-Mart now measures P&G's performance by tracking improvements in inventory turnover and stock-outs.

Joint educational programs can help break down the barriers between manufacturers and retailers. The retailing giant Royal Ahold—which owns more than 1,500 supermarkets, department stores, and other outlets in the Netherlands as well as Giant Food Stores, Bi-lo, Stop & Shop, Tops Markets, and Finast in the United States—is attempting to collaborate on an executive education program with manufacturers such as Heineken, Sara Lee Corporation, and Unilever. The program would include four or five upcoming executives from each company and focus on value-chain management.

Philip Morris runs about 20 two-day seminars annually for loyal retailers in France, where the law requires it to sell its cigarettes exclusively through 36,000 small mom-and-pop tobacconists. About 50 retailers attend each seminar, the focus of which is not on Philip Morris but on how these owners can become better retailers. Upon completion, each participant is awarded a certificate from the "Philip Morris University." The retailers are so proud of their certificates that they often display them in their stores. More important to Philip Morris, its sales and share increase at these retailers' stores.

By developing trust, manufacturers and retailers can exploit their complementary skills to reduce transaction costs, adapt quickly to marketplace changes, and develop more creative solutions to meet consumers' needs. Vertically integrated companies are too inflexible and traditional manufacturer-retailer relationships too adversarial to promote such behavior and skills. When one considers the effort it takes to manage a relationship with even one company, the competitive advantage that can flow from the ability to manage relationships with several companies is apparent. Success in rapidly changing environments will go to those who learn to make the leap of faith.

A Scale to Assess Retailer Performance

MOST MANUFACTURERS PERIODICALLY evaluate the performance of the retailers or dealers that they use to reach the market. Many manufacturers, however, depend on a single measure to make the evaluation—sales generated through the retailer or dealer. Unfortunately, this measure is not reliable, because a retailer's or dealer's location often has a major influence on how many sales it makes.

Moreover, the sales that a dealer or retailer generates are just one aspect of its performance. Understanding that fact, many manufacturers have tried to supplement sales-performance data with customer-satisfaction data for each dealer or retailer. Unfortunately, such data often is not available and can be manipulated when it is.

To provide manufacturers with another means of assessing and comparing their retailers' or dealers' performances, my colleagues and I developed a qualitative, multiple-dimension scoring system, which I call a *scale to assess retailer performance* (SARP). Although it is a more subjective measure than sales figures, it is more comprehensive. The scoring system shown here rates retailers in seven dimensions, each of which is determined by obtaining scores on three statements. Dimensions may be added or subtracted to suit a manufacturer's circumstances, and the same holds for the statements that make up each dimension. However, using too few dimensions or statements risks undermining the validity or usefulness of this type of tool.

To help reduce bias, two members of the manufacturer's organization who are familiar with the retailer being evaluated should perform the assessment.

The two people separately rate the retailer or dealer on a 7-point scale for each statement. (1=strongly disagree, 2=disagree, 3=mildly disagree, 4=neither agree nor disagree, 5=mildly agree, 6=agree, and 7=strongly agree.) Each person arrives at a score for each of the seven dimensions in the example by averaging the scores obtained for its three statements. If their scores for any statement differ greatly, they should discuss the difference and try to agree on a rating. Each calculates a total score by averaging the scores he or she obtained for the seven dimensions. Then the two total scores are averaged to produce the retailer's or dealer's final score.[3]

1. The retailer's or dealer's sales performance for us is good.

a) Over the past year, the retailer or dealer has been successful in generating high revenues for us, given the level of competition and economic growth in its market.

b) Compared with competing retailers or dealers in the district, this retailer or dealer has achieved a high level of market penetration for our products.

c) Last year, the revenues that this retailer or dealer generated for us were higher than those our other retailers or dealers within the same territory generated for us.

2. The retailer's or dealer's financial performance for us is good.

a) The cost of servicing the retailer or dealer is reasonable, given the amount of business it generates.

b) The retailer's or dealer's demands for support have resulted in adequate profits for us.

c) Over the past year, we made adequate profits from this retailer or dealer relative to the amount of time, effort, and energy that we had to devote to assisting it.

3. The retailer or dealer successfully generates growth for us.

a) The retailer or dealer will continue to be or will soon become a major source of revenue for us.

b) Over the next year, we expect the revenues this retailer or dealer generates for us to grow faster than the revenues our competitors' retailers or dealers within the same territory generate for them.

c) Over the past three years, the market share we have achieved through the retailer or dealer has grown steadily.

4. The retailer or dealer is competent.

a) The retailer or dealer has the business skills to run the kind of operation that we need.

b) The retailer or dealer demonstrates deep knowledge of the features and attributes of our products and services.

c) The retailer or dealer and its personnel have considerable knowledge of our competitors' products and services.

5. The retailer or dealer complies with channel policies, procedures, and the terms of the contract.

a) Over the past year, we have usually had success getting the retailer or dealer to participate in the following important program:_____.

b) The retailer or dealer almost always conforms to our accepted procedures.

c) The retailer or dealer usually abides by stipulations or terms and conditions contained in its contract or agreement with us.

6. The retailer or dealer adapts to marketplace changes.

a) The retailer or dealer is in touch with long-term trends in its territory and frequently adjusts its selling practices.

b) The retailer or dealer is innovative in its marketing of our products and services.

c) The retailer or dealer makes an effort to meet competitive changes in its territory.

7. **Customers are satisfied with the level and quality of services that the retailer or dealer provides in support of our products.**

   a) We rarely receive complaints about the retailer or dealer from customers.

   b) The retailer or dealer goes out of its way to make customers happy.

   c) The retailer or dealer assists customers or end users when any problems involving our products or services arise.

Two Tough Companies Learn to Dance Together

THE WORD ON THE STREET has always been that Procter & Gamble and Wal-Mart are two tough companies with whom to do business. Historically, Procter & Gamble has used its enormous power to dominate the trade. P&G would bring its breathtakingly comprehensive research on consumers to retailers and use it to argue for increased shelf space for its brands. Before retailers developed sophisticated point-of-sale systems, which generate a wealth of information on consumers, they were unable to dispute P&G's analyses and resented P&G's control over the retail trade. Over the years, P&G built up a reputation for being a "self-aggrandizing bully of the trade."[4]

For its part, Wal-Mart was renowned for demanding that its supplying manufacturers offer it rock-bottom prices, extra service, and preferred credit terms. In 1992, it instituted a policy of dealing directly with manufacturers, rendering intermediaries such as brokers and manufacturer representatives superfluous. It would do business only with vendors that invested in customized electronic-data-interchange technology and put bar codes on their products. However, because of the volume and growth Wal-Mart delivered, manufacturers had little choice but to fall into line.

Over the last ten years, however, these two giants have developed a partnership that has become the benchmark for manufacturer-retailer relationships. It is based on mutual dependence: Wal-Mart needs P&G's brands and P&G needs Wal-Mart's access to customers. The relationship took time to mature and has gone through its share of growing pains, but mutual trust has been instrumental in the companies' development of an effective long-term relationship.

In the bad old days, P&G would dictate to Wal-Mart how much P&G would sell, at what prices, and under what terms. In turn, Wal-Mart would threaten to drop P&G merchandise or give it poorer shelf locations. There was no sharing of information, no joint planning, and no systems coordination. Prior to 1987, Wal-Mart had never been contacted by a corporate officer of P&G. As Sam Walton, the founder of Wal-Mart, put it, "We just let our buyers slug it out with their salesmen."[5]

It was not until the mid-1980s that this adversarial relationship began to change. A mutual friend arranged a canoe trip for Sam Walton and Lou Pritchett, P&G's vice president for sales. On this trip, the men decided to reexamine the relationship between the two companies. They began the process by assembling the top ten officers of each company for two days to develop a collective vision of the future. Within three months, a team of 12 people from different functions in each company was established to convert that vision into an action plan. It examined how the companies could use information technology to increase sales and lower costs for both parties.

The result was a sophisticated electronic-data-interchange link, which enables P&G to take responsibility for managing Wal-Mart's inventory, of, say, P&G's Pampers disposable diapers. P&G receives continuous data by satellite on sales, inventory, and prices for different sizes of Pampers at individual Wal-Mart stores. This information allows P&G to anticipate Pampers sales at Wal-Mart, determine the number of shelf racks and quantity required, and automatically ship the orders—often directly from the factory to individual stores. Electronic invoicing and electronic transfer of funds complete the transaction cycle. Because of the speed of the entire order-to-delivery cycle, Wal-Mart pays P&G for the Pampers very shortly after the merchandise is sold to the end consumer.

This partnership has created great value for consumers in the form of lower prices and greater availability of their favorite P&G items. (Stock-outs have been virtually eliminated.) Through cooperation, superfluous activities related to order processing, billing, and payment have been eliminated; the sales representatives do not need to visit stores as often; and paperwork and opportunities for errors have been dramatically reduced. The orderless order system also means that P&G produces to demand rather than to inventory. Furthermore, Wal-Mart has succeeded in simultaneously reducing the inventory of Pampers and the probability of stock-outs, thereby avoiding lost sales for both parties. By working together, the two have turned what used to be a win-lose proposition of each striving to lower its own costs regardless of the effect on the other's costs into a win-win proposition of reduced costs and greater revenues for both parties. Wal-Mart is P&G's largest customer, generating more than $3 billion in business, which is about 10% of P&G's total revenues.

To unleash the benefits of their partnership, Wal-Mart had to trust P&G enough to share sales and price data and to cede control of the order process and inventory management to P&G. P&G had to trust Wal-Mart enough to dedicate a large cross-functional team to the Wal-Mart account, adopt everyday low prices (lower standard prices and the elimination of special promotions), and invest in a customized information link. Instead of focusing on increasing sales to Wal-Mart, the P&G team concentrates on finding ways to increase sales of P&G products to consumers through Wal-Mart and to maximize both companies' profits.

How Ekornes Turned Its Retailers into Partners

UNTIL 1993, WHEN J.E. EKORNES, a Norwegian home-furniture manufacturer, decided to overhaul its distribution system in Europe, it suffered from the problems common in traditional adversarial manufacturer-retailer relationships. Its experience in France, where it sold its products through 450 furniture dealers, was typical. A sales mentality meant that any retailer that wished to carry Ekornes's Stressless product line had access to it. Because of overdistribution, retailers did not trust Ekornes, and, in turn, Ekornes believed that the retailers were not committed to making the brand succeed. There were the usual disagreements over the support that each party was supposed to provide to the other. Meanwhile, the brand was suffering in the marketplace.

For the brand to achieve its potential, Ekornes felt it needed to work more closely with its retailers to make distribution more efficient and to increase the marketing and service support that retailers provided to the brand. So in early 1993, Ekornes decided to move away from traditional adversarial relationships to deeper, more intense relationships.

Ekornes's managers realized that there were two obstacles to developing such relationships: the inability of retailers to make satisfactory profits on the Stressless product line and the process by which Ekornes was managing its relationships with retailers. First, Ekornes focused on improving the returns to retailers, a process that meant having fewer retailers and awarding the survivors exclusive territories so that each could generate adequate sales volumes. Accordingly, over the next three years, it reduced its number of retailers in France to 150 and gave them new contracts that promised them exclusive territories. In addition, Ekornes slightly increased retailers' margins to ensure that the retailers had enough resources to support the brand with local advertising.

Ekornes also took steps to involve retailers in the change process and to make them feel like members of the Ekornes family. It arranged for them to visit its innovative factory in Norway in order to deepen their appreciation of the quality and distinctiveness of Ekornes's products. Using computerized software, it worked with retailers to figure out the optimal territory size for each. When Ekornes dropped retailers, those remaining agreed to sales goals that more than made up for the volume that would be lost by eliminating the others. At the request of the retailers, Ekornes arranged regional training sessions for the retailers' sales forces. Since the retailers were not competing with one another anymore, they were more willing to share their successful and unsuccessful sales strategies both with one another and with Ekornes's sales representatives during the training sessions.

Finally, Ekornes had to change the role of its sales force from one of selling to one of providing marketing assistance to the retailer. To do so, the company dumped the sales commission that had made up the sales force's entire pay. Instead, it began paying salespeople a fixed salary and instituted a bonus, most of which depended on the quality of the assistance that they provided to retailers.

The change process continues at Ekornes, but the results are already spectacular. Retailers have responded by increasing local advertising and dropping competing lines. Stressless sales in France have tripled over the past three years—and continue to increase at a 50% annual rate.

Notes

1. To measure trust in the various studies cited in this article, we submitted four to ten statements to the retailers. Two examples are "We can rely on the manufacturer to keep the promises it makes" and "We can count on the manufacturer to act sincerely in its dealings with us." Then we asked retailers to score on a 1-to-7 scale the degree to which they thought the statement reflected their view of the manufacturer (1=strongly disagree and 7=strongly agree). The average of the scores equaled each

retailer's level of trust in the manufacturer, with 1 representing the lowest and 7 the highest. Similar statements submitted to manufacturers were used to measure the manufacturers' trust in their retailers.

2. Ken Partch, " 'Partnering': A Win-Win Proposition. . . or the Latest Hula Hoop in Marketing?" *Supermarket Business*, May 1991, pp. 29–34.

3. For more information on how to conduct such an assessment and to test its statistical validity, see Nirmalya Kumar, Louis W. Stern, and Ravi S. Schrol, "Assessing Reseller Performance from the Perspective of the Supplier," *Journal of Marketing Research*, May 1992, pp. 238–53.

4. "Pritchett on Quick Response," *Discount Merchandiser*, April 1992, p. 64–65.

5. Sam Walton and John Huey, *Sam Walton, Made in America: My Story* (New York: Doubleday & Company, 1992), p. 186.

Originally published in November–December 1996
Reprint 96606

The author would like to thank IMD, the Marketing Science Institute, and Pennsylvania State University's Institute for the Study of Business Markets for their support of this research.

What is the Right Supply Chain for Your Product?

MARSHALL L. FISHER

Executive Summary

NEVER HAS SO MUCH TECHNOLOGY and brainpower been applied to improving supply chain performance. Point-of-sale scanners allow companies to capture the customer's voice. Electronic data interchange lets all stages of the supply chain hear that voice and react to it by using flexible manufacturing, automated warehousing, and rapid logistics. And new concepts such as efficient consumer response, accurate response, mass customization, and agile manufacturing offer models for applying the new technology.

But the performance of many supply chains has never been worse. In some cases, costs have risen to new levels because of adversarial relations between supply chain partners as well as dysfunctional industry practices such as an overreliance on price promotions. And supply chains in many industries suffer from an excess of some products and a shortage of others because of an inability to predict demand.

Why haven't the new ideas and technologies led to improved performance? Because, Marshall Fisher says, companies lack a framework for deciding which ones are best for their particular situation. Fisher offers such a framework to help managers understand the nature of the demand for their products and devise the supply chain that can best satisfy that demand.

Once products have been classified on the basis of their demand patterns, they fall into one of two categories: they are either primarily functional or primarily innovative. And each type of product requires a distinctly different kind of supply chain. The root cause of the problems plaguing many supply chains, the author contends, is a mismatch between the type of product and the type of supply chain.

NEVER HAS SO MUCH TECHNOLOGY and brainpower been applied to improving supply chain performance. Point-of-sale scanners allow companies to capture the customer's voice. Electronic data interchange lets all stages of the supply chain hear that voice and react to it by using flexible manufacturing, automated warehousing, and rapid logistics. And new concepts such as quick response, efficient consumer response, accurate response, mass customization, lean manufacturing, and agile manufacturing offer models for applying the new technology to improve performance.

Nonetheless, the performance of many supply chains has never been worse. In some cases, costs have risen to unprecedented levels because of adversarial relations between supply chain partners as well as dysfunctional industry practices such as an overreliance on price promotions. One recent study of the U.S. food industry estimated that poor coordination among supply chain partners was wasting $30 billion annually. Supply chains in many other industries suf-fer from an excess of some products and a shortage of others owing to an inability to predict demand. One department store chain

Before devising a supply-chain, consider the nature of the demand for your product.

that regularly had to resort to markdowns to clear unwanted merchandise found in exit interviews that one-quarter of its customers had left its stores empty-handed because the specific items they had wanted to buy were out of stock.

Why haven't the new ideas and technologies led to improved performance? Because managers lack a frame-work for deciding which ones are best for their particular company's situation. From my ten years of research and consulting on supply chain issues in industries as diverse as food, fashion apparel, and automobiles, I have been able to devise such a framework. It helps managers understand the nature of the demand for their products and devise the supply chain that can best satisfy that demand.

The first step in devising an effective supply-chain strategy is therefore to consider the nature of the demand for the products one's company supplies. Many aspects are important—for example, product life cycle, demand predictability, product variety, and market standards for lead times and service (the percentage of demand filled from in-stock goods). But I have found that if one classifies products on the basis of their demand patterns, they fall into one of two categories: they are either primarily functional or primarily innovative. And each category requires a distinctly different kind of supply chain. The root cause of the problems plaguing many supply chains is a mismatch between the type of product and the type of supply chain.

Is Your Product Functional or Innovative?

Functional products include the staples that people buy in a wide range of retail outlets, such as grocery stores and gas stations. Because such products satisfy basic needs, which don't change much over time, they have stable, predictable demand and long life cycles. But their stability invites competition, which often leads to low profit margins.

To avoid low margins, many companies introduce innovations in fashion or technology to give customers an additional reason to buy their offerings. Fashion apparel and personal computers are obvious examples, but we also see successful product innovation where we least expect it. For instance, in the traditionally functional category of food, companies such as Ben & Jerry's, Mrs. Fields, and Starbucks Coffee Company have tried to gain an edge with designer flavors and innovative concepts. Century Products, a leading manufacturer of children's car seats, is another company that brought innovation to a functional product. Until the early 1990s, Century sold its seats as functional items. Then it introduced a wide variety of brightly colored fabrics and designed a new seat that would move in a crash to absorb energy and protect the child sitting in it. Called Smart Move, the design was so innovative that the seat could not be sold until government product-safety standards mandating that car seats not move in a crash had been changed.

Although innovation can enable a company to achieve higher profit margins, the very newness of innovative products makes demand for them unpredictable. In addition, their life cycle is short—usually just a few months—because as imitators erode the competitive advantage that innovative products enjoy, companies are forced to introduce a steady stream of newer innovations. The short life cycles and the great variety typical of these products further increase unpredictability.

It may seem strange to lump technology and fashion together, but both types of innovation depend for their success on consumers changing some aspect of their values or lifestyle. For example, the market success of the IBM Thinkpad hinged in part on a novel cursor control in the middle of the keyboard that required users to interact with the keyboard in an unfamiliar way. The new design was so controversial within IBM that managers had difficulty believing the enthusiastic reaction to the cursor control in early focus groups. As a result, the company underestimated demand—a problem that contributed to the Thinkpad's being in short supply for more than a year.

With their high profit margins and volatile demand, innovative products require a fundamentally different supply chain than stable, low-margin functional products do. To understand the difference, one should recognize that a supply chain performs two distinct types of functions: a *physical* function and a *market mediation* function. A supply chain's physical function is readily apparent and includes converting raw materials into parts, components, and eventually finished goods, and transporting all of them from one point in the supply chain to the next. Less visible but equally important is market mediation, whose purpose is ensuring that the variety of products reaching the marketplace matches what consumers want to buy.

Each of the two functions incurs distinct costs. Physical costs are the costs of production, transportation, and inventory storage. Market mediation costs arise when supply exceeds demand and a product has to be marked down and sold at a loss or when supply falls short of demand, resulting in lost sales opportunities and dissatisfied customers.

The predictable demand of functional products makes market mediation easy because a nearly perfect match between supply and demand can be achieved. Companies that make such products are thus free to focus almost exclusively on minimizing physical costs—a crucial goal, given the price sensitivity of most functional products. To that end, companies usually create a schedule for assembling finished goods for at least the next month and commit themselves to abide by it. Freezing the schedule in this way allows companies to employ manufacturing-resource-planning software, which orchestrates the ordering, production, and delivery of supplies, thereby enabling the entire supply chain to minimize inventory and maximize production efficiency. In this instance, the important flow of information is the one that occurs within the chain as suppliers, manufacturers, and retailers coordinate their activities in order to meet predictable demand at the lowest cost.

That approach is exactly the wrong one for innovative products. The uncertain market reaction to innovation increases the risk of shortages or excess supplies. High profit margins and the importance of early sales in establishing market share for new products increase the cost of shortages. And short product life cycles increase the risk of obsolescence and the cost of excess supplies. Hence market mediation costs predominate for these products, and they, not physical costs, should be managers' primary focus.

Most important in this environment is to read early sales numbers or other market signals and to react quickly, during the new product's short life cycle. In this instance, the crucial flow of information occurs not only within the chain but also from the marketplace to the chain. The critical decisions to be made about inventory and capacity are not about minimizing costs but about where in the chain to position inventory and available production capacity in order to hedge against uncertain demand. And suppliers should be chosen for their speed and flexibility, not for their low cost.

Sport Obermeyer and Campbell Soup Company illustrate the two environments and how the resulting goals and initiatives differ. Sport Obermeyer is a major supplier of fashion skiwear. Each year, 95% of its products are completely new designs for which demand forecasts often err by as much as 200%. And because the retail season is only a few months long, the company has little time to react if it misguesses the market.

In contrast, only 5% of Campbell's products are new each year. Sales of existing products, most of which have been on the market for years, are highly predictable, allowing Campbell to achieve a nearly perfect service level by satisfying more than 98% of demand immediately from stocks of finished goods. And even the few new products are easy to manage. They have a replenishment lead time of one month and a minimum market life cycle of six months. When Campbell introduces a product, it deploys enough stock to cover the most optimistic forecast for demand in the first month. If the product takes off, more can be supplied before stocks run out. If it flops, the six-month, worst-case life cycle affords plenty of time to sell off the excess stocks.

How do goals and initiatives differ in the two environments? Campbell's already high service level leaves little room for improvement in market mediation costs. Hence, when the company launched a supply chain program in 1991 called *continuous replenishment*, the goal was physical efficiency. And it achieved that goal: the inventory turns of participating retailers doubled. In contrast, Sport Obermeyer's uncertain demand leads to high market-mediation costs in the form of losses on styles that don't sell and missed sales opportunities due to the "stockouts" that occur when demand for particular items outstrips inventories. The company's supply chain efforts have been directed at reducing those costs through increased speed and flexibility.

Although the distinctions between functional and innovative products and between physical efficiency and responsiveness to the market seem obvious once stated, I have found that many companies founder on this issue. That is probably because products that are physically the same can be either functional or innovative. For example, personal computers, cars, apparel, ice cream, coffee, cookies, and children's car seats all can be offered as a basic functional product or in an innovative form.

It's easy for a company, through its product strategy, to gravitate from the functional to the innovative sphere without realizing that anything has changed. Then its managers start to notice that service has mysteriously declined and inventories of unsold products have gone up. When this happens, they look longingly at competi-

tors that haven't changed their product strategy and
therefore have low inventories and high service. They
even may steal away the vice president of logistics from
one of those companies, reasoning, If we hire their logistics guy, we'll have low inventory and high service, too.
The new vice president invariably designs an agenda for
improvement based on his or her old environment: cut
inventories, pressure marketing to be accountable for
its forecasts and to freeze them well into the future to
remove uncertainty, and establish a rigid just-in-time
delivery schedule with suppliers. The worst thing that
could happen is that he or she actually succeeds in implementing that agenda, because it's totally inappropriate
for the company's now unpredictable environment.

Devising the Ideal Supply-Chain Strategy

For companies to be sure that they are taking the right
approach, they first must determine whether their products are functional or innovative. Most managers I've
encountered already have a sense of which products
have predictable and which have unpredictable demand:
the unpredictable products are the ones generating all
the supply headaches. For managers who aren't sure or
who would like to confirm their intuition, I offer guidelines for classifying products based on what I have found
to be typical for each category. (See the table "Functional
Versus Innovative Products: Differences in Demand.")
The next step is for managers to decide whether their
company's supply chain is physically efficient or responsive to the market. (See the table "Physically Efficient
Versus Market-Responsive Supply Chains.")

Having determined the nature of their products and
their supply chain's priorities, managers can employ a
matrix to formulate the ideal supply-chain strategy. The

four cells of the matrix represent the four possible combinations of products and priorities. (See the exhibit
"Matching Supply Chains with Products.") By using the
matrix to plot the nature of the demand for each of their
product families and its supply chain priorities, man-

Functional Versus Innovative Products: Differences in Demand

	Functional (Predictable Demand)	Innovative (Unpredictable Demand)
Aspects of Demand		
Product life cycle	more than 2 years	3 months to 1 year
Contribution margin*	5% to 20%	20% to 60%
Product variety	low (10 to 20 variants per category)	high (often millions of variants per category)
Average margin of error in the forecast at the time production is committed	10%	40% to 100%
Average stockout rate	1% to 2%	10% to 40%
Average forced end-of-season markdown as percentage of full price	0%	10% to 25%
Lead time required for made-to-order products	6 months to 1 year	1 day to 2 weeks

* The contribution margin equals price minus variable cost divided by price and is expressed as a percentage.

agers can discover whether the process the company uses for supplying products is well matched to the product type: an efficient process for functional products and

Functional products require an efficient process; innovative products, a responsive process.

a responsive process for innovative products. Companies that have either an innovative product with an efficient supply chain (upper right-hand cell) or a functional product with a responsive supply chain (lower left-hand cell) tend to be the ones with problems.

For understandable reasons, it is rare for companies to be in the lower left-hand cell. Most companies that introduce functional products realize that they need efficient chains to supply them. If the products remain functional over time, the companies typically have the good sense to stick with efficient chains. But, for reasons I will explore shortly, companies often find themselves in the upper right-hand cell. The reason a position in this cell doesn't make sense is simple: for any company with innovative products, the rewards from investments in improving supply chain responsiveness are usually much greater than the rewards from investments in improving the chain's efficiency. For every dollar such a company invests in increasing its supply chain's responsiveness, it usually will reap a decrease of more than a dollar in the cost of stockouts and forced markdowns on excess inventory that result from mismatches between supply and demand. Consider a typical innovative product with a contribution margin of 40% and an average stockout rate of 25%.[1] The lost contribution to profit and overhead resulting from stockouts alone is huge: $40\% \times 25\% = 10\%$ of sales—an amount that usually exceeds profits before taxes.

Consequently, the economic gain from reducing stockouts and excess inventory is so great that intelligent investments in supply chain responsiveness will always pay for themselves—a fact that progressive companies have discovered. Compaq, for example, decided to continue producing certain high-variety, short-life-cycle circuits in-house rather than outsource them to a low-cost Asian country, because local production gave the company increased flexibility and shorter

Physically Efficient Versus Market-Responsive Supply Chains

	Physically Efficient Process	**Market-Responsive Process**
Primary purpose	supply predictable demand efficiently at the lowest possible cost	respond quickly to unpredictable demand in order to minimize stockouts, forced markdowns, and obsolete inventory
Manufacturing focus	maintain high average utilization rate	deploy excess buffer capacity
Inventory strategy	generate high turns and minimize inventory throughout the chain	deploy significant buffer stocks of parts or finished goods
Lead-time focus	shorten lead time as long as it doesn't increase cost	invest aggressively in ways to reduce lead time
Approach to choosing suppliers	select primarily for cost and quality	select primarily for speed, flexibility, and quality
Product-design strategy	maximize performance and minimize cost	use modular design in order to postpone product differentiation as long as possible

lead times. World Company, a leading Japanese apparel manufacturer, produces its basic styles in low-cost Chinese plants but keeps production of high-fashion styles in Japan, where the advantage of being able to respond quickly to emerging fashion trends more than offsets the disadvantage of high labor costs.

That logic doesn't apply to functional products. A contribution margin of 10% and an average stockout rate of 1% mean lost contribution to profit and overhead of only .1% of sales—a negligible cost that doesn't warrant the significant investments required to improve responsiveness.

Getting Out of the Upper Right-Hand Cell

The rate of new-product introductions has skyrocketed in many industries, fueled both by an increase in the

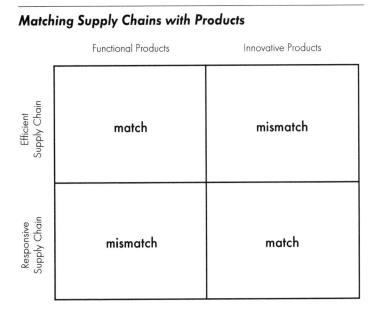

Matching Supply Chains with Products

number of competitors and by the efforts of existing competitors to protect or increase profit margins. As a result, many companies have turned or tried to turn traditionally functional products into innovative products. But they have continued to focus on physical efficiency in the processes for supplying those products. This phenomenon explains why one finds so many broken supply chains—or unresponsive chains trying to supply innovative products—in industries such as automobiles, personal computers, and consumer packaged goods.

The automobile industry is one classic example. Several years ago, I was involved in a study to measure the impact that the variety of options available to consumers had on productivity at a Big Three auto plant. As the study began, I tried to understand variety from the customer's perspective by visiting a dealer near my home in the Philadelphia area and "shopping" for the car model produced in the plant we were to study. From sales literature provided by the dealer, I determined that when one took into account all the choices for color, interior features, drivetrain configurations, and other options, the company was actually offering 20 million versions of the car. But because ordering a car with the desired options entailed an eight-week wait for delivery, more than 90% of customers bought their cars off the lot.

The dealer told me that he had 2 versions of the car model on his lot and that if neither matched my ideal specifications, he might be able to get my choice from another dealer in the Philadelphia area. When I got home, I checked the phone book and found ten dealers in the area. Assuming each of them also had 2 versions of the car in stock, I was choosing from a selection of at most 20 versions of a car that could be made in 20 million. In other words, the auto distribution channel is a kind of hourglass with the dealer at the neck. At the top of the glass, plants, which introduce innovations in color and technology every year, can provide an almost infinite variety of options. At the bottom, a multitude of customers with diverse tastes could benefit from that variety but are unable to because of dealers' practices at the neck of the glass.

The computer industry of 20 years ago shows that a company can supply an innovative product with an unresponsive process if the market allows it a long lead time for delivery. In my first job after college, I worked in an IBM sales office helping to market the System/360 mainframe. I was shocked to learn that IBM was then quoting a 14-month lead time for this hot new product. I asked how I could possibly tell a customer to wait that long. The answer was that if a customer really wanted a 360, it would wait, and that if I couldn't persuade it to wait, there must be something seriously lacking in my sales skills. That answer was actually correct: lead times of one to two years were then the norm. This meant that computer manufacturers had plenty of time to organize their supplies around physical efficiency.

There is a kind of schizophrenia in the way computer companies view their supply chains.

Now PCs and workstations have replaced mainframes as the dominant technology, and the acceptable lead time has dropped to days. Yet because the industry has largely retained its emphasis on a physically efficient supply chain, most computer companies find themselves firmly positioned in the upper right-hand cell of the matrix.

That mismatch has engendered a kind of schizophrenia in the way computer companies view their supply chains. They cling to measures of physical efficiency such as plant capacity utilization and inventory turns because those measures are familiar from their mainframe days. Yet the marketplace keeps pulling them toward measures of responsiveness such as product availability.

How does a company in the upper right-hand cell overcome its schizophrenia? Either by moving to the left on the matrix and making its products functional or by moving down the matrix and making its supply chain responsive. The correct direction depends on whether the product is sufficiently innovative to generate enough additional profit to cover the cost of making the supply chain responsive.

A sure sign that a company needs to move to the left is if it has a product line characterized by frequent introductions of new offerings, great variety, and low profit margins. Toothpaste is a good example. A few years ago, I was to give a presentation to a food industry group. I decided that a good way to demonstrate the dysfunctional level of variety that exists in many grocery categories would be to buy one of each type of toothpaste made by a particular manufacturer and present the collection to my audience. When I went to my local supermarket to buy my samples, I found that 28 varieties were available. A few months later, when I mentioned this discovery to a senior vice president of a competing manufacturer, he acknowledged that his company also had 28 types of toothpaste—one to match each of the rival's offerings.

Does the world need 28 kinds of toothpaste from each manufacturer? Procter & Gamble, which has been simplifying many of its product lines and pricing, is coming to the conclusion that the answer is no. Toothpaste is a product category in which a move to the left—from innovative to functional—makes sense.

In other cases when a company has an unresponsive supply chain for innovative products, the right solution is to make some of the products functional and to create a responsive supply chain for the remaining innovative products. The automobile industry is a good example.

Many suggestions have been made for fixing the problems with the auto distribution channel I have described here, but they all miss the mark because they propose applying just one solution. This approach overlooks the fact that some cars, such as the Ford Fairmont, are inherently functional, while others, such as the BMW Z3 roadster (driven in the James Bond movie *Golden Eye*), are innovative. A lean, efficient distribution channel is exactly right for functional cars but totally inappropriate for innovative cars, which require inventory buffers to absorb uncertainty in demand. The most efficient place to put buffers is in parts, but doing so directly contradicts the just-in-time system that automakers have so vigorously adopted in the last decade. The just-in-time system has slashed parts inventories in plants (where holding inventory is relatively cheap) to a few hours, while stocks of cars at dealers (where holding inventory is expensive) have grown to around 90 days.

Efficient Supply of Functional Products

Cost reduction is familiar territory, and most companies have been at it for years. Nevertheless, there are some new twists to this old game. As companies have aggressively pursued cost cutting over the years, they have begun to reach the point of diminishing returns within their organization's own boundaries and now believe that better coordination across corporate boundaries—with suppliers and distributors—presents the greatest opportunities. Happily, the growing acceptance of this view has coincided with the emergence of electronic networks that facilitate closer coordination.

Campbell Soup has shown how this new game should be played. In 1991, the company launched the continuous-replenishment program with its most progressive retailers. The program works as follows: Campbell establishes electronic data interchange (EDI) links with retailers. Every morning, retailers electronically inform the company of their demand for all Campbell products and of the level of inventories in their distribution centers. Campbell uses that information to forecast future demand and to determine which products require replenishment based on upper and lower inventory limits previously established with each retailer. Trucks leave the Campbell shipping plant that afternoon and arrive at the retailers' distribution centers with the required replenishments the same day. The program cut the inventories of four participating retailers from about four to two weeks of supply. The company achieved this improvement because it slashed the delivery lead time and because it knows the inventories of all retailers and hence can deploy supplies of each product where they are needed the most.

Pursuing continuous replenishment made Campbell aware of the negative impact that the overuse of price promotions can have on physical efficiency. Every January, for example, there was a big spike in shipments of Chicken Noodle Soup because of deep discounts that Campbell was offering. Retailers responded to the price cut by stocking up, in some cases buying a year's sup-

ply—a practice the industry calls *forward buying.*
Nobody won on the deal. Retailers had to pay to carry the
year's supply, and the shipment bulge added cost
throughout the Campbell system. For example, chicken-
boning plants had to go on overtime starting in October
to meet the bulge. (See the graph "How Campbell's Price
Promotions Disrupted Its Supply System.") Recognizing
the problem, Campbell required its retail customers on
the continuous-replenishment program to waive the
option of forward buying at a discounted price. A retailer
that promotes Campbell products in its stores by offering a discounted price to consumers has two options: it
can pay Campbell an "everyday low price" equal to the
average price that a retailer receiving the promotional
deals would pay or it can receive a discount on orders
resulting from genuine increases in sales to consumers.

The Campbell example offers some valuable lessons.
Because soup is a functional product with price-sensitive
demand, Campbell was correct to pursue physical efficiency. Service—or the in-stock availability of Campbell
products at a retailer's distribution center—did increase
marginally, from 98.5% to 99.2%. But the big gain for the
supply chain was in increased operating efficiency,
through the reduction in retailers' inventories. Most
retailers figure that the cost of carrying the inventory of a
given product for a year equals at least 25% of what they
paid for the product. A two-week inventory reduction
represents a cost savings equal to nearly 1% of sales.
Since the average retailer's profits equal about 2% of
sales, this savings is enough to increase profits by 50%.

Because the retailer makes more money on Campbell
products delivered through continuous replenishment, it
has an incentive to carry a broader line of them and to
give them more shelf space. For that reason, Campbell

found that after it had introduced the program, sales of its products grew twice as fast through participating retailers as they did through other retailers. Understandably, supermarket chains love programs such as Campbell's. Wegmans Food Markets, with stores in upstate New York, has even augmented its accounting system so that it can measure and reward suppliers whose products cost the least to stock and sell.

There is also an important principle about the supply of functional products lurking in the "everyday low price" feature of Campbell's program. Consumers of functional products offer companies predictable demand in exchange for a good product and a reasonable price.

How Campbell's Price Promotions Disrupted Its Supply System

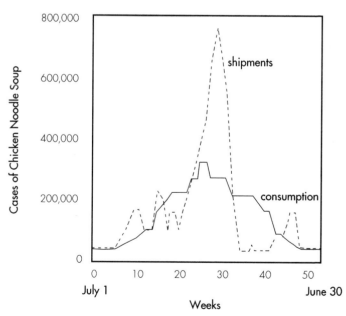

The challenge is to avoid actions that would destroy the inherent simplicity of this relationship. Many companies go astray because they get hooked on overusing price promotions. They start by using price incentives to pull demand forward in time to meet a quarterly revenue target. But pulling demand forward helps only once. The next quarter, a company has to pull demand forward again just to fill the hole created by the first incentive. The result is an addiction to incentives that turns simple, predictable demand into a chaotic series of spikes that only add to cost.

Campbell Soup has shown how manufacturers and retailers can cooperate to cut costs throughout the system.

Finally, the Campbell story illustrates a different way for supply chain partners to interact in the pursuit of higher profits. Functional products such as groceries are usually highly price-sensitive, and negotiations along the supply chain can be fierce. If a company can get its supplier to cut its price by a penny and its customer to accept a one-cent price increase, those concessions can have a huge impact on the company's profits. In this competitive model of supply chain relations, costs in the chain are assumed to be fixed, and the manufacturer and the retailer compete through price negotiations for a bigger share of the fixed profit pie. In contrast, Campbell's continuous-replenishment program embodies a model in which the manufacturer and the retailer cooperate to cut costs throughout the chain, thereby increasing the size of the pie.

The cooperative model can be powerful, but it does have pitfalls. Too often, companies reason that there never can be too many ways to make money, and they decide to play the cooperative and competitive games at the same time. But that tactic doesn't work, because the two approaches require diametrically different behavior. For example, consider information sharing. If you are my supplier and we are negotiating over price, the last thing you want to do is fully share with me information about your costs. But that is what we both must do if we want to reduce supply chain costs by assigning each task to whichever of us can perform it most cheaply.

Responsive Supply of Innovative Products

Uncertainty about demand is intrinsic to innovative products. As a result, figuring out how to cope with it is the primary challenge in creating a responsive supply process for such products. I have seen companies use four tools to cope with uncertainty in demand. To fashion a responsive supply process, managers need to understand each of them and then blend them in a recipe that's right for their company's particular situation.

Although it may sound obvious, the first step for many companies is simply to *accept* that uncertainty is inherent in innovative products. Companies that grew up in an oligopoly with less competition, more docile customers, and weaker retailers find it difficult to accept the high levels of demand uncertainty that exist today in many markets. They have a tendency to declare a high level of forecast errors unacceptable, and they virtually command their people to think hard enough and long enough to achieve accuracy in their forecasts. But these companies can't remove uncertainty by decree. When it comes to innovative products, uncertainty must be accepted as good. If the demand for a product were predictable, that product probably would not be sufficiently innovative to command high profit margins. The fact is that risk and return are linked, and the highest profit margins usually go with the highest risk in demand.

Once a company has accepted the uncertainty of demand, it can employ three coordinated strategies to manage that uncertainty. It can continue to strive to *reduce* uncertainty—for example, by finding sources of new data that can serve as leading indicators or by having different products share common components as much as possible so that the demand for components becomes more predictable. It can *avoid* uncertainty by cutting lead times and increasing the supply chain's flexibility so that it can produce to order or at least manufacture the product at a time closer to when demand materializes and can be accurately forecast. Finally, once uncertainty has been reduced or avoided as much as possible, it can *hedge against* the remaining residual uncertainty with buffers of inventory or excess capacity. The experiences of National Bicycle, a subsidiary of Matsushita Electric, and of Sport Obermeyer illustrate the different ways in which these three strategies can be blended to create a responsive supply chain.

National Bicycle prospered for decades as a small but successful division. But by the mid-1980s, it was in trouble. Bicycles in Japan were functional products bought mainly as an inexpensive means of transportation, and sales were flat. Bicycles had become a commodity sold on the basis of low price, and Japan's high labor costs left National Bicycle unable to compete with inexpensive bikes from Taiwan and Korea.

In 1986, in an attempt to salvage the situation, Matsushita appointed as president of National an executive from another division who had no experience in bicycles.

The new president, Makoto Komoto, saw that the division had many strengths: technical expertise in manufacturing and computers, a highly skilled workforce, a strong brand name (Panasonic), and a network of 9,000 dealers. Komoto also noticed that National Bicycle had an innovative product segment that enjoyed high profit margins: sports bicycles that affluent customers bought purely for recreation. He concluded that National's only hope was to focus on that segment and use the division's strengths to develop a responsive chain that could supply sports bikes while avoiding the high risk of overproduction that resulted from their short life cycle and uncertain demand.

According to Komoto's vision, a customer would visit a Panasonic dealership and choose a bike from a selection of 2 million options for combining size, color, and components, using a special measuring stand to find the exact size of the frame that he or she needed. The order would be faxed to the factory, where computer-controlled welding equipment and skilled workers would make the bike and deliver it to the customer within two weeks.

National Bicycle's success is a good example of a responsive supply chain achieved through avoiding uncertainty.

Komoto's radical vision became a reality in 1987. By 1991, fueled by this innovation, National Bicycle had increased its share of the sports bicycle market in Japan from 5% to 29%. It was meeting the two-week lead time 99.99% of the time and was in the black.

National Bicycle's success is a good example of a responsive supply chain achieved through avoiding uncertainty. National has little idea what customers will order when they walk into a retail shop, but that doesn't matter: its produce-to-order system allows it to match supply with demand as it happens. By radically increasing the number of choices from a few types of bikes to 2 million, it can induce the customer to sacrifice immediate availability and wait two weeks for a bicycle.

National's program is part of a new movement called *mass customization*: building the ability to customize a large volume of products and deliver them at close to mass-production prices. Many other companies have found that they, too, can benefit from this strategy. For example, Lutron Electronics of Coopersburg, Pennsylvania, became the world leader in dimmer switches and other lighting controls by giving customers an essentially unlimited choice of technical and fashion features. Says Michael W. Pessina, Lutron's vice president of manufacturing operations, "With our diverse product line, customer demand can be impossible to predict. Yet by configuring products at the time of order, we can offer customers tremendous variety and fill orders very quickly without having to stock a huge amount of inventory."

Mass customization is not without its challenges. For example, what does National Bicycle do with its plant during the winter, when no one is buying bikes? It builds an inventory of high-end sports bicycles. In addition, mass customization is not necessarily cheap. National's custom production requires three times more labor than assembly-line mass production of bikes. Interestingly, one of the main reasons why Henry Ford in the early 1900s moved in the opposite direction—from craft to mass production—was to slash labor costs, which he succeeded in doing by a factor of three. So what has changed to make custom production viable now? Affluent consumers are willing to pay for high-margin, innovative products; and those products require a different, more expensive, but more responsive production process than the functional Model T did.

Sport Obermeyer, which is based in Aspen, Colorado, designs and manufactures fashion skiwear and distributes it through 800 specialty retailers located throughout the United States. Because 95% of its products are new each year, it constantly faces the challenges and risks of demand uncertainty: stockouts of hot styles during the selling season and leftover inventory of "dogs" at the end of the season. In 1991, the company's vice president, Walter R. Obermeyer, launched a project to attack those problems by blending the three strategies of reducing, avoiding, and hedging against uncertainty. To reduce uncertainty, Sport Obermeyer solicited early orders from important customers: the company invited its 25 largest retailers to Aspen each February to evaluate its new line. Sport Obermeyer found that the early orders from this handful of retailers permitted it to forecast national demand for all its products with a margin of error of just 10%.

Although it was helpful to get this information several months before Sport Obermeyer was required to ship its products in September, it didn't solve the company's problem, because long lead times forced it to commit itself to products well before February. Obermeyer concluded that each day shaved off the lead time would save the company $25,000 because that was the amount it spent each day at the end of September shipping products by air from plants in Asia to have them in stores by early October—the start of the retail season. Once that figure was announced to employees, they found all kinds of ways to shorten the lead time. For example, the person who had dutifully used standard mail service to get design information to the production manager in Hong Kong realized that the $25 express-mail charge was a bargain compared with the $25,000 per day in added costs resulting from longer lead times caused by mail delays. Through such efforts, Sport Obermeyer was able to avoid uncertainty on half of its production by committing that production after early orders had been received in February.

Nevertheless, the company still had to commit half of the production early in the season, when demand was uncertain. Which styles should it make then? It would stand to reason that they should be the styles for which Sport Obermeyer had the most confidence in its forecasts. But how could it tell which those were? Then the company noticed something interesting. Obermeyer had asked each of the six members of a committee responsible for forecasting to construct a forecast for all products, and he used the average of the six forecasts as the company's forecast. After one year of trying this method, the company found that when the six individual forecasts agreed, the average was accurate, and when they disagreed, the average was inaccurate. This discovery gave Sport Obermeyer a means of selecting the styles to make early. Using this information as well as data on the cost of overproduction and underproduction, it developed a model for hedging against the risk of both problems. The model tells the company exactly how much of each style to make early in the production season (which begins nearly a year before the retail season) and how much to make in February, after early orders are received.

Sport Obermeyer's approach, which has been called *accurate response*, has cut the cost of both overproduction and underproduction in half—enough to increase profits by 60%. And retailers love the fact that the system results in more than 99% product availability: they have ranked Sport Obermeyer number one in the industry for service. (See "Making Supply Meet Demand in an Uncertain World," by Marshall L. Fisher, Janice H. Hammond, Walter R. Obermeyer, and Ananth Raman, HBR May–June 1994.)

Companies such as Sport Obermeyer, National Bicycle, and Campbell Soup, however, are still the exceptions. Managers at many companies continue to lament that although they know their supply chains are riddled with waste and generate great dissatisfaction among customers, they don't know what to do about the problem. The root cause could very well be a misalignment of their supply and product strategies. Realigning the two is hardly easy. But the reward—a remarkable competitive advantage that generates high growth in sales and profits—makes the effort worth it.

Note

1. The contribution margin equals price minus variable cost divided by price and is expressed as a percentage. This type of profit margin measures increases in profits produced by the incremental sales that result from fewer stockouts. Consequently, it is a good way to track improvements in inventory management.

Originally published in March–April 1997
Reprint 97205

Make Your Dealers Your Partners

DONALD V. FITES

Executive Summary

A DECADE AGO, many observers predicted Caterpillar's demise. Yet today the company's overall share of the world market for construction and mining equipment is the highest in its history. And the biggest reason for the turnaround, writes Caterpillar's chairman and CEO Donald Fites, has been the company's system of distribution and product support and the close customer relationships it fosters.

The backbone of that system is Caterpillar's 186 independent dealers around the world. They have played a central role in helping the company build close relationships with customers and gain insights into how it can improve products and services.

How did Caterpillar build such a strong network of dealers? Fites attributes the company's success to several factors. For one thing, the company stands by its dealers in goods times and in bad. In addition, it gives them extraordinary support, helps ensure that the dealerships are well run, and emphasizes full and honest two-way communication. Finally, Fites stresses the emotional ties that have developed between Cat and its dealers over time.

The tight working relationships that Caterpillar has forged with its dealers hold important lessons for managers at other manufacturers. In many manufacturing industries, distribution and product support remain underappreciated strategic assets, but that status will soon change, contends Fites. Engineering excellence, manufacturing efficiency, and quality are rapidly becoming the ante to get into the game. Over the next 10 to 20 years, companies will need superb distribution systems capable of providing outstanding customer support if they are to prevail in the global economy.

A DECADE AGO, MANY observers predicted that Caterpillar would join the long list of U.S. corporations that had fallen to the Japanese. Doomsayers on Wall Street, at business schools, and in the press focused particularly on the rivalry between Caterpillar and Komatsu. With Komatsu boasting tremendous cost advantages (as much as 40% in some product lines) and excellent products, they accepted as a foregone conclusion that Komatsu would fulfill its vow to "encircle Cat" and become the dominant producer in our industry.

Like many predictions, this one fell short. Despite determined efforts by Komatsu, Hitachi, Kobelco, and others, our overall share of the world market for construction and mining equipment is the highest in our history. We have maintained our strong position in Japan through Shin Caterpillar Mitsubishi, our 33-year-old joint venture with Mitsubishi Heavy Industries. And after suffering some fearsome losses in 5 of the 11 years from 1982 through 1992, we have rebounded financially with record profits and a return on equity in the mid to high thirties.

I'm often asked how Caterpillar rose to the challenge. Several factors played a part. They include the tremendous value of our brand name; the excellent quality of our products; the high resale value of our machines; a reorganization of the corporation to push decision making down into the organization to make the company flatter, leaner, and more responsive to customers' needs; big investments to revamp and streamline manufacturing operations, resulting in the most competitive factories in our industry; more frequent and timely new-product introductions; a heightened focus on costs; and the weakening of the dollar relative to the yen.

But the biggest reason for Caterpillar's success has been our system of distribution and product support and the close customer relationships it fosters. Don't get me wrong: We think we are better engineers and manufacturers than our competitors. But we are convinced that our single greatest advantage over our competition was and still is our system of distribution and product support. The backbone of that system is our 186 independent dealers around the world who sell and service our machines and diesel engines. They have played a pivotal role in helping us build and maintain close relationships with customers and gain insights into how we can improve our products and services to better fill customers' needs.

Many features of Caterpillar's distribution system are tailored to meet the unique characteristics of our industry. For instance, our industry's sales volume is relatively low: Global sales of earthmoving equipment average 200,000 to 300,000 units per year. A relatively small number of dealers sell those machines. Even though we might customize some features, such as the operator's cab or the paint job, the same standard product can be sold throughout the world. The machines are expensive, but they stay in service for 10 to 12 years on average; many operate for 20 to 30 years. And finally, because these products operate in extremely tough environments, even the best-made, most durable machines wear out and have parts that must be rebuilt or replaced, which requires an organization that can service products quickly to minimize downtime.

Nevertheless, I believe the tight working relationships we have forged with our independent dealers to meet our customers' needs hold lessons for other manufacturers of relatively standard big-ticket products that require after-sales service and support. The lessons include the following:

- Local dealers who are long-established members of their communities can get closer to customers than a global company can on its own; but to tap the full potential of such dealers, a company must forge extremely close ties with them and integrate them into its critical business systems. When treated in this way, dealers can serve as sources of market information and intelligence, as proxies for customers, as consultants, and as problem solvers. Indeed, our dealers play a vital role in almost every aspect of our business, including product design and delivery, service and field support, and the management of replacement-part inventories.

- Dealers can be much more than a channel to customers. They can play an important role in providing customers with a wide range of services before and after the sale. Those services include advice on the selection and application of a product, financing, insurance, operator training, maintenance and repair, and help in deciding when it makes economic sense to replace a machine.

- Creating an outstanding distribution organization requires significant investments by both the company and its independent dealers. Although those investments take the usual forms of money and capital assets, they also include softer assets such as training and developing a common understanding of what it takes to provide superior customer service.

- The quality of the relationship between a company and its dealers is much more important than the contractual agreements or the techniques and tactics that make the relationship work on the surface. What matters is mutual trust, and that is fostered by observing a few simple rules: Share gain as well as pain; strive for continuity in relationships and consistency in policies; and communicate constantly. For a company that relies on independent dealers to present one face to its customers around the world, it must have uniform practices and performance standards for dealers and treat them all with equal consideration while recognizing that they are independent and unique in many ways.

- When a company is deciding which new products to add to its line, it should consider two key factors: First, which new product contenders best fit its distribution system, and second, whether the distribution system will add value to the product in the eyes of the end user.

In most manufacturing industries, distribution and product support remain underappreciated strategic assets. That situation will soon change because the global winners over the next 10 to 20 years are going to be the companies with the best distribution organizations that also provide superb customer support. Engineering excellence, manufacturing efficiency, and quality are rapidly becoming givens; everyone is going to need them to be a player. Indeed, most companies deficient in those areas have already disappeared.

Although many Japanese companies had the early advantage in manufacturing excellence, U.S. companies may have the edge this time around. Why? Because they know more about distribution than anyone else. Whether we're talking about financial services or servicing products, U.S. companies have a real strength in service. So this is a revolution they can really capitalize on if they treat distribution as if it were as integral to their businesses as product design and manufacturing. That's one reason I feel very bullish about my own company. We know how to do it. We have already built true partnerships with our dealers.

Quite frankly, distribution traditionally has not been a strength of Japanese companies. Marketing people and salespeople historically have been looked down upon in Japanese society. I saw that firsthand when I lived there in the 1970s. We worked diligently with Mitsubishi Heavy Industries, our joint venture partner, to help them understand the importance that we placed on the distribution side of our business. At the time, a sales position just didn't have the same status in the social or company hierarchy as an engineering or accounting position. I think that feeling still prevails in many Japanese companies.

Many companies do not put a great deal of emphasis on after-sales service. One possible reason for that in Japan is that the automobile and consumer electronics industries (and many others) strive to make their products so well that they don't require parts or service. That approach, however, just

We'd sooner cut off our right arm than sell directly to customers and bypass our dealers.

doesn't work in our business, where machines are subjected to intense use. Caterpillar's approach to product design and support recognizes this fact. A critical design criterion for our machines is that they can be repaired economically and conveniently. And our highly integrated manufacturing and distribution systems are designed so that we can replace a part in any machine anywhere in the world within 48 hours. In the vast majority of cases, our dealers can provide the replacement part on the spot. Our competitors cannot match that kind of consistent performance; it is not unusual for one of their customers to have to wait four or five days for a part.

One possible reason for the disparity is that few companies have integrated their dealers into their business systems to the degree we have. Everyone in the business world talks about the importance of the trust that exists between Japanese manufacturers and their suppliers.

But, in our industry, I don't see that same level of trust in their relationships with their distributors.

It is not uncommon for our competitors to bypass their distributors and sell directly to the customer if they think a deal is important enough. We'd sooner cut off our right arm than do that. Caterpillar sells directly to customers only in the newly opened markets of formerly socialist countries and to original-equipment manufacturers and the U.S. government. And in almost all those cases, our dealers, not the company, provide the after-sales service and support.

OVER THE YEARS, people have said to me, "Isn't it expensive to have all those independent dealers? Couldn't you make more money if you distributed and serviced Caterpillar machines yourself?" I have always answered that the knowledge of the local market and the close relations with customers that our dealers provide are worth every penny. Our independent dealer in Novi, Michigan, or in Bangkok, Thailand, knows so much more about the requirements of customers in those locations than a huge corporation like Caterpillar could. Our dealers tend to be prominent business leaders in their service territories who are deeply involved in community activities and who are committed to living in the area. Their reputations and long-term relationships are important because selling our products is a personal business. As a result, Caterpillar never appears as a remote presence or as the overseas branch of a foreign multinational. (Two-thirds of our dealerships are located outside North America, and the vast majority are privately held companies.)

After a product leaves our door, the dealers take over. They are the ones on the front line. They're the ones who live with a product for its lifetime. They're the ones the customers see. Although we offer financing and insurance, they arrange those deals for the customers. They're out there making sure that when a machine is delivered, it's in the condition it's supposed to be in. They're out there training a customer's operators. They service a product frequently throughout its life, carefully monitoring a machine's health and scheduling repairs to prevent costly downtime.

The customer, the end user, knows that there is a $16 billion-plus company called Caterpillar. But the dealer creates the image of a company that doesn't just stand behind its products but *with* its products anywhere in the world. Our dealers are the reason that our motto—Buy the Iron, Get the Company—is not an empty slogan.

A piece of construction equipment or a heavy-duty engine is a major capital asset, and owners want a healthy return on their investment. Many of our customers will pay a premium for machines they can count on. For example, high in the mountains on the Indonesian province of Irian Jaya, Freeport-McMoRan operates one of the largest copper and gold mines in the world, 24 hours a day, 365 days a year. At an altitude of more than 13,000 feet, the mine is accessible only by aerial cableway or helicopter, and the ore is slurried through pipelines to loading docks along the coast. The operation relies on more than 500 pieces of Caterpillar mining and construction equipment—a total investment worth several hundred million dollars—including loaders, track-type tractors, and mammoth 240-ton, 2,000-plus-horsepower trucks. Many of these machines cost well over $1 million apiece. The mine also depends on Caterpillar diesel-engine generators as its sole source of electric power. If this equipment breaks down for any length of time, the company doesn't move ore. When that happens, it loses money, and fast.

At the other end of the spectrum, the stakes are also high for the small-business owner or independent contractor whose livelihood depends on a $50,000, 79-horsepower backhoe loader. If that machine doesn't function, work doesn't get done, deadlines are missed, related tasks have to be rescheduled, customers and subcontractors get angry, reputations are affected, opportunities open up for competitors, and money is lost.

To put it succinctly, our mission is to convince customers that our company and our distribution organization are the best ones to keep their equipment running in top condition. They have to believe that thanks to the way we design, manufacture, and service our machines, they will have a higher percentage of uptime than they would with a competitor's product; thus they can reduce costs and make more money than they could using another company's equipment.

Obviously, Caterpillar bears great responsibility for designing and manufacturing equipment that is durable and easily repaired, and over the past decade, we have greatly improved our equipment in this regard. We have made our systems more modular so that when, for example, a transmission needs to be serviced or repaired, it can be removed much more quickly than before. And to speed the process further, it often will be replaced with a new or remanufactured exchange transmission from a dealer's parts inventory.

Caterpillar also has developed the fastest and most comprehensive parts-delivery system in any industry that I'm aware of. Although we have long guaranteed delivery of any part anywhere in the world within 48 hours, our dealers now provide more than 80% of the parts a customer wants immediately. And Caterpillar ships more than 99% of the parts that a dealer does not have on hand the same day the order is placed. Compare that to the automobile industry, in which the average wait for a part that a dealer does not have in stock is likely to be from two to seven days. Moreover, we have maintained this performance during a period—the last ten years—when the number of parts that we service has more than doubled because of explosive growth in our product line. In the past five years alone, we have completely revamped our product line; in 1995, we introduced 49 new models, more than twice the number we introduced in 1991.

We maintain 22 parts facilities around the world, with more than 10 million square feet of warehouse storage. We service 480,000 line items (different part numbers), of which we stock 320,000. (Caterpillar's and its suppliers' factories make the remaining 160,000 on demand.) We ship 84,000 items per day, or about one per second every day of the year.

In addition, our dealers, each of whom typically stocks between 40,000 and 50,000 line items, have made huge investments in parts inventories, warehouses, fleets of trucks, service bays, diagnostic and service equipment, sophisticated information technology, and highly trained people. Indeed, our dealers, whose investments in their individual businesses range from $10 million to more than

We are putting in place a system to deliver part before customers realize they need them.

$100 million, collectively surpass our might. Their combined net worth is about $5 billion, or about 1.5 times Caterpillar's stockholders' equity. They collectively employ 73,600 people, about 19,000 more than Caterpillar. And while their average revenues are about $150 million, several dealers have annual revenues in the neighborhood of $1 billion.

It is somewhat misleading, however, to talk about "us" and "them," because we genuinely treat our system and theirs as one. Our joint distribution operations are all linked by a worldwide computer network. I can turn to the computer on my desk and find out how many machines in the world are waiting for a part. On this particular day, it's about 1,300, which is pretty good considering that there are hundreds of thousands of Caterpillar machines out there.

But we aren't resting on our laurels. We are now putting in place an information system that will permit us to deliver a part *before* a customer even realizes that he or she needs it. The system will monitor machines remotely and notify the local dealer when a part is beginning to show signs of an impending failure so that we can arrange to replace it before it fails. (See the insert "Making Global Connections at Caterpillar.")

SIGNIFICANTLY, CATERPILLAR DOES NOT view its distribution system as a one-way channel from the factory to the customer. Rather, information about the customer constantly feeds back into the system and drives new product development and enhancements in service.

For example, a dealer advisory group recently helped us fine-tune the design of a new line of motor graders under development. It pointed out that if the graders were manufactured according to the original design, people would get mud on their pants when reaching for a toolbox; moreover, operators taller than six feet two would hit their heads when they stood up if the side panel was raised to service or repair the machine. In response, we changed the location of the toolbox and redesigned the panel so that it opens sideways.

We also work with dealers to survey every purchaser of a Cat machine at least three times during the first two years after the sale. In addition, we survey customers about delivery of parts and service. (We send out nearly 90,000 surveys each year and get a response rate of about 40%.) The data is enormously useful both to the company and to dealers because it enables us to refine our targets and strive for constant improvement along a variety of dimensions. For example, the survey results helped persuade some dealers to change their inventory practices to ensure that they always had the full range of batteries and fan belts on hand.

We also involve dealers and customers in programs on product quality, cost reduction, and other manufacturing issues. Our Partners in Quality program, for example, links personnel at a factory responsible for building a particular machine with people at selected high-volume dealerships. They meet quarterly to discuss quality issues. In addition, those dealers audit each machine they receive from the plant, and if there's something wrong, they feed that information back to the plant immediately. The idea is to catch problems as early as we can—ideally, before they become problems the customer sees.

For example, one dealer discovered that hoses in a new model of motor grader had been installed incorrectly. When the dealer alerted the factory in Decatur, Illinois, we retrained the assembler, fixed the machines still in the factory, and notified other dealers to fix the machines that we had already shipped, thus correcting the problem before any machines had gone to customers.

Similarly, our dealer in Thailand felt that a pump in a new line of hydraulic excavators was not durable enough for the rigors to which it was being subjected in that part of the world. The dealer persuaded us to use a different pump on the machines until we could redesign the one in question.

Besides helping us manufacture better products, our dealer network also generates extraordinary and timely market intelligence. It's a rich source of information that enables us to introduce new products and support services successfully. We were especially thankful for that network when we introduced the D9L track-type tractor in the early 1980s.

The D9L, a machine weighing well over 100,000 pounds, is used primarily in mining and heavy construction. It was one of our first tractors to utilize a new design: an elevated sprocket that alters the shape of the track undercarriage from a traditional oval to a triangle. The new design achieves a variety of objectives: improved traction, reduced stress on the undercarriage and other fast-wearing parts, easier and faster repairs, and improved productivity. Accordingly, we priced the machine above competitors' tractors that had more traditional designs.

We began shipping the D9L in 1981. Our timing was hardly great. The U.S. mining industry was in the doldrums. To make matters worse, Komatsu had recently entered the U.S. market with aggressive pricing and a particular focus on mining customers; it was also trying to penetrate the Middle East, another major opportunity for the D9L.

In mid-1982, when we had several hundred machines operating throughout the world, a potential disaster struck. As the machines approached 2,500 hours of operation, they began to fail. It turned out that a variety of parts—ranging from undercarriage components to water pumps to fan drives—were not as durable as we had thought. Our dealers quickly identified and reported the problems, and within weeks after the first machines had failed, we realized that we were facing a major crisis. The reputation of the D9L, customers' acceptance of the new design, and our leadership in the large-tractor business were at stake.

Our dealers then helped us create and implement a comprehensive program for repairing machines, replacing the culprit parts in machines that had not yet failed, and assuring unhappy customers that we were on top of the problem. For instance, several dealers, including Whayne Supply, based in Louisville, Kentucky, and Bowmaker (now Finning) in the United Kingdom, assigned some of their mechanics to serve on SWAT teams that repaired the machines quickly—often during the night. Bowmaker dispatched teams of mechanics to assist Zahid, our dealer in Saudi Arabia. And Whayne quickly provided extraordinary service that prevented some important mining customers in Kentucky and southern Indiana from bolting to competitors.

By mid-1983, just a year after we had first learned of the problems, virtually all the D9Ls had been repaired. The result: We minimized downtime, customer dissatisfaction evaporated, the D9L turned into a popular product, and the elevated-sprocket tractor gave us an overwhelming advantage.

Even if Caterpillar is not the first to market with a product, our dealer network allows the company to be a fast follower. For instance, our distribution system made it possible for us to become one of the leading players in backhoe loaders, a business we entered in the mid 1980s. A backhoe loader is a small tractor with a hydraulic boom and excavation bucket mounted on the rear of the vehicle, and a loader bucket in front. Like hydraulic excavators, the machines are versatile

When considering which new products to add, we always ask how we can leverage our distribution system.

and used for many different kinds of work. They are especially popular with building-construction and utility contractors, who were not our traditional customers.

After a rocky start, we have established a strong sales position, surging past several entrenched competitors to capture the number two position in the worldwide industry. It was not just our product but also our dealers that made those gains possible. Not only did they invest in inventories of replacement parts needed to support the new product, they also invested sizable sums in rental fleets when it became clear that many small contractors preferred to rent, rather than buy, the machines. In addition, they aggressively added salespeople to call on these smaller customers, with whom we hadn't traditionally had much contact.

On the other hand, we are careful not to misuse our distribution system. We don't design and manufacture something and then think about distribution; instead, we consider it a critical part of our value equation. Because we understand the competitive advantage provided by our dealers, the first questions we always ask when considering which new products to add are, How else can we leverage our distribution system around the world, and can our system add value? If the answer to the latter is yes, then customers, dealers, and Caterpillar will all benefit. That's why we got into truck engines and the big 6,000-kilowatt generator sets. And that's one of the reasons we recently entered the agricultural equipment business with our rubberbelted Challenger series of tractors.

We haven't changed; the agricultural equipment business has, and now it fits our distribution organization. Thirty or 40 years ago, manufacturers needed a mom-and-pop dealership in every town to compete. That is no longer true. The farmers out there today are sophisticated businesspeople. They don't care whether there's a dealer in their hometown; they'll buy from centers within 150 miles of their farms when they can get products of superior technology and the high level of service and parts support that our dealers offer. And so we see a real growth opportunity in agricultural equipment.

Highway-truck engines provide another case in point. Although we sell these engines directly to original-equipment manufacturers, our dealers invest time and money to influence truck owners to ask for Cat engines. That makes sense for all involved because parts-and-service support for our engines is conducted by or channeled through Caterpillar dealers. Once again, our distribution system adds value and the end user benefits.

W E HAVE GOOD RELATIONSHIPS with dealers not just because they like us but because the investment is good for them and for Caterpillar, and because both parties work to strengthen the relationship. Both parties invest heavily in maintaining a relationship built on trust, confidence, and shared interests and rewards. The rules don't change, so everyone knows what to expect of one another. We expect our dealers to be industry leaders, to provide the best customer support, and to demonstrate leadership in their communities. And they expect the highest-value products and services from us.

I hear a lot of talk about trust between manufacturers and their suppliers and distributors, but few companies really put the talk into practice. The kind of trust that exists between Caterpillar and its dealers is something that could be built up only over generations. Our dealership agreements are documents that run just a few pages. They have no expiration date, and either party can terminate without cause on 90 days' notice. But turnover is rare because we recognize that we're in this together. The final decision either to terminate or to appoint any dealer in the world rests with the CEO of this company; no one else at Caterpillar can make that decision.

We won't bypass our dealers in good times for short-term gain or turn on them in bad times to avoid short-term pain.

The foundation of our relationship is that both sides profit from their respective investments in the distribution system. Our dealers are entrepreneurs who know how to make money. They also know very well that Caterpillar is much more than just a good account—we are a valuable long-term business associate.

Our tight relationships are based on a handful of principles and practices. They include the following:

We don't gouge our dealers. When times get tough, many companies turn on their dealers to prop up their own profits. Similarly, when a particularly lucrative opportunity presents itself, many companies will try to grab all the riches for themselves. We won't bypass our dealers for short-term gain or turn on them to avoid short-term pain.

During the 1970s, when the Alaskan pipeline was built, the pipeline consortium demanded that we sell directly to them or else they would buy from our competitors. We refused. In the end, the consortium did buy our equipment—from a joint venture between our Alaskan dealer and a Missouri dealer with a proven record of performance serving pipeline customers.

Even more telling are the sacrifices we made to keep our distribution organization financially viable during the 1980s and during an industry slump in the early 1990s. Caterpillar's challenges during the 1980s stemmed from the collective impact of several trends. The energy shock that followed the Iranian revolution triggered a deep global recession that affected customers in every part of the world; unit sales in the industry dropped about 40% around the world in one year. Japanese and European competitors aggressively targeted North America. Compounding Caterpillar's difficulties, our costs were too high, the value of the dollar began to soar, especially against the yen, and competitors were establishing higher standards for manufacturing and product development processes. We had work to do.

But it wasn't our dealers' fault that we were not more competitive. We didn't want them to bear the brunt of our problems, so we decided to shoulder most of the burden. Strategically, that was the right thing to do, but it was painful. For three straight years—1982, 1983, and 1984—we lost about a million dollars a day, or $953 million in total. But I don't think we lost a single dealer around the world.

We weren't being altruistic. We needed our dealers to defend our market leadership. We understood that if we let Komatsu or any other competitor erode our position in the United States, Europe, Asia, or anywhere else, it would cost us five times as much to get it back as it would to defend it. That is the difference between taking a long-term view of business and taking a short-term view.

Our approach was vindicated when the industry recovered. For example, every one of our five dealers in Mexico survived that terrible period. Our competitors' dealers struggled and many failed. When the good times returned, we were the only ones with a viable dealer organization in Mexico, and we got the vast majority of the business and still have it.

We have continued to operate in the same way. We again protected our dealers when our markets slumped in the early 1990s. In the United States, for example, our dealers remained financially sound throughout the recession and were able to order machines in advance of the upturn in late 1993. In contrast, many of our competitors' dealers went out of business or were financially zapped during the slump and could not get the financing they needed to buy machines.

We give our dealers extraordinary support. On the face of it, much of the support that we offer dealers may not sound unusual. Like other manufacturers, Caterpillar helps its dealers finance purchases by customers. It supports dealers in inventory management and control, logistics, equipment management, and maintenance programs. For example, we have long supplied our dealers with sophisticated software that incorporates some of the best practices in those areas. The company also publishes a huge volume of technical material each year and underwrites technical training and support for dealers' personnel in such areas as managing quality, continuous improvement, benchmarking, cost management, and communications. And we are prepared to respond to any need for training that a dealer identifies, whether it be in planning, forecasting, information systems, marketing and advertising, or other business functions.

We also give our dealers wholehearted support when one of our competitors zeroes in on a territory and tries to create a beachhead by offering dramatically low prices. Sometimes that means helping our dealer meet the competition by offering lower prices. At other times, it means helping the dealer fight back with a marketing campaign emphasizing that a Cat machine's lifetime cost is much lower than a competitor's. In still other situations, it might mean helping the dealer cut costs.

> *When we see particular dealers not performing well, we jump in and help them. We want dealers to succeed.*

We ensure that our dealerships are well run.   Every year, we review all our dealers' performance—in terms of sales, market position, service capability, organizational structure, and plans for ownership and management continuity—to establish the areas that each dealer needs to work on during the next year. In addition, finance people in each of our sales regions review the dealerships' financials with their principals on a semiannual basis.

When we see particular dealers not performing well, we jump in and help them. We take poor performance seriously—we want dealers to succeed. We'll show a dealer how his or her financial and operating ratios stack up against those of comparable dealers, because generally it's something internal that makes one less profitable than another—such as sloppy inventory management, not enough service people, or too much overhead. We will help him or her develop programs to improve the operation's profitability.

Although it is a rare occurrence, the hardest situation is when the problem really is the owner's poor leadership. Even in those cases, we won't sit on the sidelines. We try to find a solution that the owner can accept. Maybe it's bringing in a new partner. Maybe it's giving a son or daughter a chance. Maybe it's hiring an outsider to run the business until someone else in the family is ready. Whatever the solution, we will not simply watch while a dealership declines.

We communicate fully, frequently, and honestly.
There are no secrets between our dealers and us. We have the financial statements and key operating data of every dealer in the world. Dealers wouldn't give us that information if they didn't trust us. In addition, virtually all Caterpillar and dealer employees have real-time access to continually updated databases of service information, sales trends and forecasts, customer satisfaction surveys, and other critical data.

As you would with all valuable business associates, we take pains to keep the dealers fully informed about the key issues facing the company. Top-level Caterpillar managers meet annually with key people from the dealerships at regional conferences, where we discuss our sales goals for each product line and what each party has to do to achieve them. In addition, we periodically invite all 186 dealers to a weeklong conference in Peoria for a comprehensive review of strategy, product plans, and marketing policies.

There is also a lot of routine contact between people at the dealerships and people at all levels of Caterpillar. At lower levels, there is daily communication. But it's also not unusual for dealers' principals and senior corporate staff to speak several times a week. In the last five years in particular, we have made a conscious effort to increase the exposure of people in our organization to dealers. Our reorganization in 1990 from functional groups into profit centers greatly increased our contacts with dealers. Virtually everyone from the youngest design engineer to the CEO now has contact

I'm not reluctant to tell dealers what I think they're doing wrong. And they are not reluctant to tell us where we are lacking.

with somebody in our dealer organizations. We recognize the tremendous value of the market knowledge that our dealers gain from being on the front lines every day with our customers.

We believe strong business relationships are personal. It would be easy for an outside observer to assume that the structures we have created—the annual conferences, the strategy meeting, the profit centers, and the dealer advisory councils—are the backbone of the relationship with our dealers. But the form is the easy part. What caused the deep relationships to develop are the close personal ties that have been nurtured. Those ties form a kind of family relationship.

When I see Chappy Chapman, a retired executive vice president who was my boss for a long time, out on the golf course, he always asks about particular dealers or about their children, who may be running the business now. And every time I see those dealers, they inquire, "How's Chappy?" That's the sort of relationship we have.

Dealers can call me or any senior corporate officer at any time, and they do. Virtually any dealer in the world is free to walk in my door. I'll know how much money he made last year and his market position. And I'll know what is happening in his family. I consider the majority of dealers personal friends. Of course, one reason I know the dealers so well is that I rose through our distribution organization. But my predecessors, who had a variety of backgrounds, understood the importance of distribution, too.

Don't get me wrong. There's no dealer worshiping around here. I say they're personal friends, but I'm not reluctant to tell them what I think they're doing wrong in their service territories. And they are not reluctant to tell us where we are lacking. If you're unsure of each other, you can't have that kind of honest give-and-take.

We strive to keep dealerships in the family.   Continuity reinforces mutual trust, limits disputes, encourages sharing of information, and generates larger gains for everyone. To that end, we prefer to work with privately held enterprises, which typically enjoy longer-term management continuity than public companies.

The CEO's tenure at many public companies is five or six years at most. That is not long enough for us. As I noted, the average life span of a piece of construction equipment is 10 to 12 years, and many machines operate for 20 to 30 years. In addition, many of our customers are privately held concerns that value long-term personal relationships.

On average, our dealerships have remained in the hands of the same family or company for more than 50 years. Some of these relationships, including many overseas, predate the 1925 merger that created Caterpillar. And, with rare exceptions, these dealers derive 90% or more of their revenue from selling and supporting our products; for many, it's 100%. From the company's early years, we have believed that an individual with most of his or her wealth tied up in a Caterpillar dealership is going to do a better job than somebody who has little or nothing at risk.

We actively help dealers keep the business in the family. For example, when the principal of a privately held dealership is about 50 years old, we hold seminars for the family on tax issues and succession planning—both financial and management. These seminars are held two or three times during the principal's active working life to ensure that the next generation is ready.

We also take proactive steps to try to interest children of dealership owners in the business. We recently held a conference in Peoria that was attended by 20 to 25 sons and daughters, who ranged in age from 15 to 23. The idea was to introduce them to Caterpillar, to get them interested in the business, and to allow them to meet their peers. We took them to the plants. We let them operate machines. And we talked to them about what we expect of dealer principals.

We also encourage owners to involve their kids in their dealerships from an early age. We help owners orchestrate a range of summer jobs and then full-time jobs when their children graduate from college. We might suggest that a dealer have a son or daughter work as a parts salesperson for two years, then run the engine business, and next be put in charge of product support. In that way, when the principals are ready to retire, we have seen enough of their children to know what they can do and which ones are capable of taking over the business.

We also strive for management continuity at the small number of Caterpillar dealerships owned by public companies. For example, we encourage their boards to establish long CEO tenures, and we push them to take succession planning seriously.

O F   C O U R S E ,   O U R   R E L A T I O N S H I P S with our dealers are not perfect. The boundaries of service territories, product and pricing policies, and our preference that dealers shun diversification can be sources of friction. But we think we are better than most companies at resolving such conflicts. That's because of our mutual interests and the respect Caterpillar managers and dealers hold for one another. It is also because of our emotional commitment to the business and to one another.

I have worked for Caterpillar for 39 years and have held jobs all over the world. I love the equipment we sell. I feel great when I'm out on a construction job watching our equipment work. It's real. You can be proud of it. It looks good. It performs well. If you look around at the highway system you drive on, the water that flows into your home, the electricity that is supplying you with power, chances are our equipment made it possible somewhere along the way. Plenty of Caterpillar managers and dealers share my feelings.

I'm not so naïve as to think that people would invest their fortunes in a dealership if they did not believe they were going to get an attractive return. But I think there's more to it than that. What people understand about being a Caterpillar dealer is that it transcends the financial reward. There's a camaraderie among our dealers around the world that really makes it more than just a financial arrangement. They feel that what they're doing is good for the world because they are part of an organization that makes, sells, and tends to the machines that make the world work.

Making Global Connections at Caterpillar

Steven E. Prokesch

IMAGINE THE FOLLOWING scenario. A part on a Caterpillar machine operating at a copper mine in Chile begins to deteriorate. A district center that continuously monitors the health of all the Caterpillar machines in its area by remotely reading the sensors on each machine automatically spots a problem in the making and sends an electronic alert to the local dealer's field technician through his portable computer. The message tells him the identity and location of the machine and sends his computer the data that sparked the alert and its diagnosis. Then, with the aid of the computer, the technician validates the diagnosis and determines the service or repair required, the cost of labor and parts, and the risks of not performing the work.

The technician's computer also tells him exactly which parts and tools he will need to make the repair. Then, with a touch of a key, the technician ties into Caterpillar's worldwide information system, which links dealers, Caterpillar's parts-distribution facilities, Cat's and its suppliers' factories, and large customers' inventory systems. He instantly determines the best sources of the parts and the times when each source can deliver them to the dealer's drop-off point.

Next, the technician sends a proposal to the customer by computer or phone, and the customer tells him the best time to carry out the repair. With a few more keystrokes, the technician orders the parts. The electronic order instantly goes to the factories or warehouses that can supply the parts in time. At the factories and warehouses, the message triggers the printing of an order ticket and perhaps automatically sets into motion an automated crane that retrieves the parts from a storage rack. Soon the parts are on their way to the dealer's pick-up site.

Within hours of the initial alert, the technician is repairing the machine. An interactive manual on his computer guides him, providing him with the latest best-practice procedures for carrying out the repair. The repair completed, the technician closes the work order, prints out an invoice, collects by credit card, and electronically updates the machine's history. That information is added to Caterpillar's databases, which helps the company spot any common problems that a particular model might have and thereby continually improve its machines' designs.

Sound like science fiction? It isn't. Caterpillar hopes to have such a system capable of monitoring all its machines around the world within several years. Most of the pieces are already in place: the sensors in the machines; computers that diagnose problems and instruct technicians in how to make repairs; and the information system that ties together Caterpillar's factories, distribution centers, dealers, and large customers. The system currently links some 1,000 locations across 23 time zones and 160 countries.

Only two pieces are missing: the remote monitoring system and the worldwide sharing of inventories by Caterpillar and its dealers and suppliers. But even those pieces are within reach, Caterpillar executives say. Indeed, Cat is already testing a prototype of the monitoring system.

The global information system is a critical part of Caterpillar's drive to expand its industry-leading position by minimizing the downtime and cost of operating and servicing its machines. The system promises to help Caterpillar and its dealers do an even better job of heading off major machine failures. For example, it will help a dealer spot and repair a transmission before it has been ruined and needs to be totally replaced.

Another obvious advantage is that by treating their inventories as one, Caterpillar and its suppliers, dealers, and customers will be able to slash their combined inventories significantly. (Caterpillar and its dealers currently have a total of about $2 billion worth of parts in their inventories.) Even bigger savings could flow from reductions in the time that technicians require to diagnose and repair machines. "The amount of time that will be saved is probably in the range of 20% to 30%," says James W. Baldwin, vice president of the Parts and Service Support Division. "When you consider that field service workers are billed out at $20 to $50 an hour, that's a significant savings."

With Caterpillar's models proliferating and becoming more complex, and with business outside the United States accounting for more than half its sales, the company believes that its ambitious information system is a necessity, not a luxury. "It is as important for the mechanic at a dealership in New Delhi to be able to walk over to his interactive computer screen and get the information on how to service a new model as it is for a mechanic at a dealership in San Francisco," says Donald V. Fites, Caterpillar's chairman.

Adds Baldwin: "We're spending in excess of $250 million on the system, and that does not include our dealers' investments. That is a lot of money for our competitors to try to match. Will they be able to copy our system eventually? Sure, it's possible, but it will take them considerable time. And we'll continue to move ahead, making it tough for them to catch up."

Originally published in March–April 1996
Reprint 96206

From Value Chain to Value Constellation

Designing Interactive Strategy

RICHARD NORMANN AND
RAFAEL RAMÍREZ

Executive Summary

IN TODAY'S FAST-CHANGING competitive environment, strategy is no longer a matter of positioning a fixed set of activities along that old industrial model, the value chain. Successful companies increasingly do not just *add* value, they *reinvent* it. The key strategic task is to reconfigure roles and relationships among a constellation of actors—suppliers, partners, customers—in order to mobilize the creation of value by new combinations of players.

What is so different about this new logic of value? It breaks down the distinction between products and services and combines them into activity-based "offerings" from which customers can create value for themselves. But as potential offerings grow more complex, so do the relationships necessary to create them. As a result, a company's strategic task becomes the ongoing reconfiguration and integration of its competencies and customers.

185

The authors provide three illustrations of these new rules of strategy. IKEA has blossomed into the world's largest retailer of home furnishings by redefining the relationships and organizational practices of the furniture business.

Danish pharmacies and their national association have used the opportunity of health care reform to reconfigure their relationships with customers, doctors, hospitals, drug manufacturers, and with Danish and international health organizations to enlarge their role, competencies, and profits.

French public-service concessionaires have mastered the art of conducting a creative dialogue between their customers—local governments in France and around the world—and a perpetually expanding set of infrastructure competencies.

STRATEGY IS THE ART OF creating value. It provides the intellectual frameworks, conceptual models, and governing ideas that allow a company's managers to identify opportunities for bringing value to customers and for delivering that value at a profit. In this respect, strategy is the way a company defines its business and links together the only two resources that really matter in today's economy: knowledge and relationships or an organization's competencies and customers.

But in a fast-changing competitive environment, the fundamental logic of value creation is also changing and in a way that makes clear strategic thinking simultaneously more important and more difficult. Our traditional thinking about value is grounded in the assumptions and the models of an industrial economy. According to this view, every company occupies a position on a value chain. Upstream, suppliers provide inputs. The company then adds value to these inputs, before passing them downstream to the next actor in the chain, the customer (whether another business or the final consumer). Seen from this perspective, strategy is primarily the art of positioning a company in the right place on the value chain—the right business, the right products and market segments, the right value-adding activities.

Today, however, this understanding of value is as outmoded as the old assembly line that it resembles and so is the view of strategy that goes with it. Global competition, changing markets, and new technologies are opening up qualitatively new ways of creating value. The options available to companies, customers, and suppliers are proliferating in ways Henry Ford never dreamed of.

Of course, more opportunities also mean more uncertainty and greater risk. Forecasts based on projections from the past become unreliable. Factors that have always seemed peripheral turn out to be key drivers of change in a company's key markets. Invaders from previously unrelated sectors change the rules of the game overnight.

In so volatile a competitive environment, strategy is no longer a matter of positioning a fixed set of activities along a value chain. Increasingly, successful companies do not just *add* value, they *reinvent* it. Their focus of strategic analysis is not the company or even the industry but the *value-creating system* itself, within which different economic actors—suppliers, business partners, allies, customers—work together to *co-produce* value. Their key strategic task is the *reconfiguration* of roles and relationships among this constellation of actors in order to mobilize the creation of value in new forms and by new players. And their underlying strategic goal is to create an ever-improving fit between competencies and customers.

To put it another way, successful companies conceive of strategy as systematic social innovation: the continuous design and redesign of complex business systems.

IKEA: The Wealth of Realizing New Ideas

For an example of what this means, consider the story of IKEA's transformation from a small Swedish mail-order furniture operation into the world's largest retailer of home furnishings. In an industry where few companies move beyond their home-country base, IKEA has created a global network of more than 100 stores. In 1992, these stores were visited by 96 *million* people and generated revenues of $4.3 billion. They have made IKEA into a growth and profit engine with an average annual growth rate of 15% over the past 5 years and profit margins that outside observers estimate at 8% to 10%, high enough to allow the company to expand without going to the stock exchange for funding.

By now, the key elements of IKEA's winning business formula are well known: simple, high-quality, Scandinavian design; global sourcing of components; knock-down furniture kits that customers transport and assemble themselves; huge suburban stores with plenty of parking and amenities like coffee shops, restaurants, even day-care facilities. A portion of what IKEA saves on low-cost components, efficient warehousing, and customer self-service it passes on to customers in the form of lower prices, anywhere from 25% to 50% below those of its competitors.

But to focus on IKEA's low costs and low prices is to miss the true significance of the company's business innovation. IKEA is able to keep costs and prices down because it has systematically redefined the roles, relationships, and organizational practices of the furniture business. The result is an integrated business system that invents value by matching the various capabilities of participants more efficiently and effectively than was ever the case in the past.

Start with IKEA's relationship to its customers. The company offers customers something more than just low prices. It offers a brand new division of labor that looks something like this: if customers agree to take on certain key tasks traditionally done by manufacturers and retailers—the assembly of products and their delivery to customers' homes—then IKEA promises to deliver well-designed products at substantially lower prices.

Every aspect of the IKEA business system is carefully designed to make it easy for customers to take on this new role. For example, IKEA prints more than 45 million catalogues every year in 10 different languages. Though each catalogue features only 30% to 40% of the company's roughly 10,000 products, every copy becomes a "script," explaining the roles each actor performs in the company's business system.

So too with the company's stores. Free strollers, supervised child care, and playgrounds are available for children, as well as wheelchairs for the disabled and elderly. There are cafés and restaurants so customers can get a quick bite to eat. The goal is to make IKEA not just a furniture store but a family-outing destination.

At the front door, customers are supplied with catalogues, tape measures, pens, and notepaper to help customers make choices without the aid of salespeople.

Products are grouped together to offer not just chairs and tables but designs for living. In addition, each item carries simple readable labels with the name and price of the product; the dimensions, materials, and colors in which it is available; instructions for care; and the location in the shop where it can be ordered and picked up. After payment, customers place their packages in carts to take them to their cars. If the package won't fit, IKEA will even lend or sell at cost an automobile roof rack.

IKEA wants its customers to understand that their role is not to *consume* value but to *create* it. IKEA offers families more than co-produced furniture, it offers co-produced improvements in family living—everything from interior design to safety information and equipment, insurance, and shopping as a form of entertainment.

To call these services amenities is to underestimate their central significance to IKEA's strategic intent: to understand how customers can create their own value and to create a business system that allows them to do it better. IKEA's goal is not to *relieve* customers of doing certain tasks but to *mobilize* them to do easily certain things they have never done before. Put another way, IKEA invents value by enabling customers' own value-creating activities. As one company brochure puts it, "Wealth is [the ability to] realize your ideas."

To mobilize its customers to create value, IKEA must similarly mobilize its 1,800 suppliers, located in more than 50 countries around the world. In order to keep its side of the work-sharing bargain, IKEA must find suppliers that can offer both low costs and good quality. It takes enormous care to find and evaluate potential suppliers and to prepare them to play their role in the IKEA business system. Thirty buying offices around the world seek out candidates. Then designers in the centralized design office at IKEA's operational headquarters in Älmhult, Sweden, who work two to three years ahead of current product, decide which suppliers will provide which parts.

Once part of the IKEA system, long-term suppliers not only gain access to global markets but also receive technical assistance, leased equipment, and advice on bringing production up to world quality standards. This effort got started in the early 1960s, when IKEA began to purchase components from Polish manufacturers. Today IKEA works with some 500 suppliers in Eastern Europe. There, as elsewhere, the company plays a major role in improving the business infrastructure and manufacturing standards of its partners.

For example, the company employs about a dozen technicians in a unit called IKEA Engineering to provide suppliers with technical assistance. The company's Vienna-based Business Service Department runs a computer database that helps suppliers find raw materials and introduces them to new business partners.

Finally, what is true for IKEA's relationships with customers and suppliers is also true for its internal business processes, which it designed to mirror and support the logic of the whole value-creating system. A good example is IKEA's highly efficient logistics system.

The company's insistence on low costs from its suppliers has two important implications. First, the sourcing of components is widely dispersed. The back and seat of a chair may be made in Poland, the legs in France, and the screws that hold it all together in Spain. Second, the company must order parts in high volumes. Both factors make it imperative for IKEA to have an efficient system for ordering parts, integrating them into products, and delivering them to stores—all the while minimizing the costs of inventory.

The centerpiece of this system is IKEA's world network of 14 warehouses. The largest, 135,000 square meters in Älmhult, holds enough items to furnish 30,000 three-bedroom apartments. Most ordering is done electronically. Cash registers at IKEA stores around the world relay sales information to the nearest warehouse as well as to operational headquarters in Älmhult, where information systems oversee and analyze sales and shipping patterns worldwide.

Big as they are, these warehouses are much more than simple storage facilities. Instead, they operate as logistical control points, consolidation centers, and transit hubs. They play a proactive role in the integration of supply and demand, reducing the need to store production runs for long peri-

IKEA is more than a link on a value chain. It is the center of a constellation of services, goods, and design.

ods, holding unit costs down, and helping retail stores to anticipate needs and eliminate shortages.

The image of a value chain fails to capture the complexity of roles and relationships in the IKEA business system. IKEA did *not* position itself to add value at any one point in a predetermined sequence of activities. Rather, IKEA set out systematically to reinvent value and the business system that delivers it for an entire cast of economic actors. The work-sharing, co-productive arrangements the company offers to customers and suppliers alike force both to think about value in a new way—one in which customers are also suppliers (of time, labor, information, and transportation), suppliers are also customers (of IKEA's business and technical services), and IKEA itself is not so much a retailer as the central star in a constellation of services, goods, design, management, support, and even entertainment. The result: IKEA has succeeded, arguably, in creating more value per person (customer, supplier, and employee) and in securing greater total profit from and for its financial and human resources than all but a handful of other companies in any consumer industry.

The New Logic of Value

IKEA's extraordinary business innovation is made possible by a fundamental transformation in the way that value is created. But what is this new logic of value, and what are its strategic implications for today's managers?

To answer these questions, begin with the simple observation that any product or service is really the result of a complicated set of activities: myriad economic transactions and institutional arrangements among suppliers and customers, employees and managers, teams of technical and organizational specialists. In fact, what we usually think of as products or services are really frozen activities, concrete manifestations of the relationships among actors in a value-creating system. To emphasize the way all products and services are grounded in activity, we prefer to call them offerings.

Every economic revolution redefines the roles and relationships on which offerings are based. This was true during the industrial revolution when technological breakthroughs in the application of energy to useful work made possible the factory system with its highly specialized division of labor. Today, under the impact of information technology and the resulting globalization of markets and production, new methods of combining activities into offerings are producing new opportunities for creating value.

One implication of this phenomenon is that the very distinction between physical products and intangible services is currently breaking down. Does IKEA offer a product or a service? The answer is neither—and both. Very few offerings can be clearly defined as one or the other anymore. Increasingly, they involve some complex combination of the two roles.

Take the simple example of an economic transaction familiar to everyone: a cash withdrawal from one's bank account. Not so long ago, this transaction was clearly a service, a personal exchange between a customer, who went to his or her local bank, and a teller, who fulfilled the customer's request for cash. But in the last decade, this traditional service has been completely transformed by the application of information technology.

Today the vast majority of cash withdrawals take place by means of automatic teller machines (ATMs). This change has reconfigured the transaction in two directions. First, the customer engages in a self-service activity not so different from the role of the buyer of IKEA furniture. Second, a great deal of attention, expertise, and activity is now devoted to the design, building, and maintenance of self-service support tools: the cash machines themselves, the plastic cards used by customers to access the machines, the computer networks connecting the machines to the bank's information and accounting systems.

This is not merely a change in technology or even in the transaction itself. It is a change in the entire value-creating system. The scene, the script, the roles of the relevant actors have all been transformed. When ATMs were first introduced, some observers questioned whether customers would play their assigned part. Critics even speculated that customers would resist this attempt by banks to burden them with extra work, that customers would insist on retaining the personal interaction with the teller.

Such criticisms missed the point and for a simple reason. The reconfiguration of the cash-withdrawal transaction offered customers a qualitatively new kind of value. In particular, it eliminated traditional constraints of space and time. No longer do customers have to go to their local bank branch during business hours. They can get cash at any time and, with the proliferation of ATM networks, pretty much anywhere. Thus the vast majority of customers flocked to ATMs and adapted to them quickly and easily. So much so that, today, few remember the long lines that used to form at banks on Friday afternoons as depositors rushed to cash their payroll checks or get money for the weekend.

What is so different about this new kind of value? One useful way to describe it is that value has become more *dense.* Think of density as a measure of the amount of information, knowledge, and other resources that an economic actor has at hand at any moment in time to leverage his or her own value creation. Value has become more dense in

The goal is not to create value for customers but to mobilize customers to create their own value from the company's various offerings.

that more and more opportunities for value creation are packed into any particular offering. A visit to an IKEA shop is not just shopping but entertainment. ATMs allow people not just to get cash but to get it anytime and nearly anywhere. A Swatch watch allows its owner not only to tell time but also to make a fashion statement (which explains why the average Swatch customer in Italy owns six).

The new logic of value presents companies with three strategic implications :

- First, in a world where value occurs not in sequential chains but in complex constellations, the goal of business is not so much to make or do something of value for customers as it is to mobilize customers to take advantage of proffered density and create value *for themselves*. That is why ATMs are so popular despite the critics. And that is why IKEA has become the world's largest furniture retailer. To put it another way, companies do not really compete with one another anymore. Rather, it is offerings that compete for the time and attention and money of customers.

- Second, what is true for individual offerings is also true for entire value-creating systems. As potential offerings become more complex and varied, so do the relationships necessary to produce them. A single company rarely provides everything anymore. Instead, the most attractive offerings involve customers and suppliers, allies and business partners, in new combinations. As a result, a company's principal strategic task is the reconfiguration of its relationships and business systems.

- Third, if the key to creating value is to co-produce offerings that mobilize customers, then the only true source of competitive advantage is the ability to conceive the entire value-creating system and make it work. IKEA creates more value because it mobilizes more activities—of customers and suppliers. It reshuffles activities among actors so that actor and activity are better matched. To win, a company must write the script, mobilize and train the players, and make the customer the final arbiter of success or failure. To go *on* winning, a company must create a dialogue with its customers in order to repeat this performance over and over again and keep its offerings competitive.

Companies create value when they make not only their offerings more intelligent but their customers (and suppliers) more intelligent as well. To do this, companies must continuously reassess and redesign their competencies and relationships in order to keep their value-creating systems malleable, fresh, and responsive. In the new logic of value, this dialogue between competencies and customers explains the survival and success of some companies and the decline and failure of others.

Danish Pharmacies: Reconfiguring Business Systems

The new logic of value, and the dialogue between competencies and customers that it creates, presents every company with a stark choice: either reconfigure its business system to take advantage of these trends or be reconfigured by more dynamic competitors.

To exploit these trends, managers must take a number of steps. To begin with, they must reconsider the business potential of their chief assets: the company's knowledge base and its customer base. Then they must reposition or reinvent the company's offerings to create a better fit between the company's competencies and the value-creating activities of its customers. Finally, they need to make new business arrangements and, sometimes, new social and political alliances to make these offerings feasible and efficient.

Consider the example of a business that at first glance may seem anything but a promising candidate for business-system redesign: Denmark's network of 300 privately owned pharmacies. Just over ten years ago, Denmark, like many other European countries, began to reform and deregulate its state-funded health care system in an effort to put a brake on rising costs.

Danish pharmacies are privately owned but nonetheless heavily regulated. For centuries, they have enjoyed a legal monopoly on the sale of both over-the-counter and prescription drugs. In addition, the pharmacies have had the right to manufacture generic drugs and thus the means to compete with their suppliers on everything except patented pharmaceuticals.

The other side of the coin is that the Danish state sets pharmaceutical prices and that it does so in a negotiation that looks at drug margins in the context of overall pharmacy profits. Until recently, this negotiation was annual, which meant that if pharmacy profits suddenly rose, then the state would cut drug prices the following year to bring profits back into line and share this "windfall" with the taxpayers. In practice, pharmacy profits *never* rose or fell very much in the old days, because, while the system guaranteed a high degree of security, it did nothing at all to encourage efficiency, innovation, or gains in productivity.

Decades of this system also left the pharmacies highly vulnerable to competition if they ever lost their monopoly. Worse yet, the movement to control health care costs had prompted a call in several quarters for outright nationalization of the pharmacies in order to make regulation complete.

So when the political system began to focus on health care, the pharmacies and their professional organization, the Danish Pharmaceutical Association, thought they saw the handwriting on the wall—an altered industry, new competitors, new dangers—and decided to take a hard look at their assets to see if they could find new opportunities as well. They concluded that their network of local pharmacies had two potential but so-far underutilized strengths.

The first was the corps of local pharmacists themselves, who were well-educated health care professionals. (Of course in Denmark, as elsewhere in the West, most critical decisions about patient health care were made by other actors in the system: primarily the physicians who wrote prescriptions and the pharmaceutical companies that developed new drugs.)

A pharmacy could be more than a place to buy drugs. It could be a comprehensive source of health information.

The second strength was the fact that the network of 300 pharmacies and 1,600 subsidiary outlets throughout the country represented a highly effective access channel to the Danish population. People respected and trusted their local pharmacists. What's more, as the general public became better informed, people began to see that good health was not something they could delegate to the government or the health care industry. Health depended on personal behavior and individual lifestyle choices. The public was hungry for information and advice on how to live a healthier life.

These two strengths gave the pharmacists an opportunity to reposition their offerings and redefine their business. A pharmacy could be more than a place to buy prescription drugs and other pharmaceutical products. It could become a comprehensive source of health care information and services.

This redefinition of its business led the Association to adopt three interconnected goals: to develop pharmacies into a more advanced knowledge and service business; to establish a solid, productive relationship with government health care agencies; and to reorganize the Association along lines that would help to achieve goals one and two.

Alongside these articulated aims, the Association had several tacit goals. For one thing, it meant to do everything possible to preserve its monopoly in pharmaceuticals retailing and its strong position in wholesaling. For another, it wanted to lower operating costs and increase pharmacy productivity—and to get legislation enacted that would give pharmacies some incentive to work more efficiently.

Efficiency had had a low priority for Danish pharmacies ever since the advent of strict state regulation. In setting prices, the state had always allowed for a modest profit. There had never been any reason to streamline operations. That now changed. If deregulation was coming, the Association would need to compete more effectively on every front, and it now sought a new legal environment that would allow it to benefit from its own efforts to improve efficiency and expand services.

In 1984, the Danish parliament changed the law. The state would set prices for two years at a time; if pharmacies could generate higher margins than predicted, they could keep the difference, at least until the next negotiation. Immediately, the pharmacies began to rationalize operations and cut staff. Net profits rose dramatically, with periodic setbacks as the Ministry of Health lowered prices.

At about this same time, the Association took two other steps to strengthen its position. First, in an effort to undercut attacks on its monopoly in drug retailing, the Association tried to downplay its direct competition with the pharmaceutical industry by setting up a subsidiary to do its drug manufacturing. Second, it managed to emerge from a series of mergers in pharmaceuticals wholesaling with a 25% controlling interest in a wholesaling giant that had 70% of the market.

Meanwhile, the pharmacists went to work on their retailing operation. In essence, the pharmacies wanted to broaden their traditional approach, delivery of conventional pharmaceutical "hardware" (in other words, selling drugs), into a concept they called Pharmaceutical Care, which would emphasize the "software" portion of health care delivery. They saw Pharmaceutical Care as a way of carving out and legitimizing a strong position within the health care system and, at the same time, of gaining access to the core of their customers' value-creating activities in health maintenance.

Beginning in 1982 and continuing into the 1990s, the pharmacies and their national association devised and carried out a series of strategies that sought to involve private customers and health care institutions in new relationships and offerings.

They expanded their range of products to include health and diet foods, high-quality herbal medicines, skin-care and other items, and they worked with suppliers to develop new quality-control measures and informational labeling.

They upgraded their customer-information services, installed computers to access health information, and published and distributed self-help books and preventive health care pamphlets.

They initiated their own antitobacco campaign and started selling literature and antismoking chewing gum. In 1986, they began offering stop-smoking courses that combined education and group therapy.

They developed a computer database on pharmaceutical interactions and side effects and installed a computer prescription service and an electronic pharmaceutical ordering system.

They developed home health care packages for newly discharged hospital patients, self-care packages for routine health problems such as measuring blood-pressure, support packages for health care institutions, and preventive-care packages for customers with special nutritional or dietary needs.

These strategies met with limited success, at least in the beginning.

In fact, the pharmacies had set themselves a difficult task. They were trying to protect their monopoly in pharmaceutical retailing; improve their position in wholesaling; take on a more central role in drug training, education, and quality control; and greatly enlarge their activities in health counseling, preventive medicine, and the sale of herbals, health food, and diet products. The other players in the health care industry tended to see these latter goals in particular as encroachments on their own exclusive preserves. It did not help that, in the midst of this seemingly predatory expansionism, the pharmacists were making bigger net profits than ever before in their history.

The Association had to guard its monopoly, enlarge its role in counseling and preventive medicine, increase sales—and step on no one's toes.

The Association saw all this in quite a different light, of course. After decades of strategic hibernation, the pharmacists were rising to the business and social challenges of fundamental health care reform. Indeed, given their history, they showed themselves surprisingly ready and able to modernize their operations, update their expertise, redefine their customer base, rethink their business, and tailor a fresh fit between competencies and customers both new and old.

Customers were not up to so much sudden change; doctors and hospitals met innovation with suspicion and resistance.

It was just that neither the state nor the customers themselves were quite up to so much sudden change. The state moved so slowly in deregulating and reforming Danish health care (84% of health care is still in the public sector) that the Association's innovations kept running into regulatory barriers and political pitfalls. And the customers that the Association had thought to mobilize around its new concept of holistic, preventive health maintenance—doctors, hospitals, long-term care facilities, even patients—tended to greet proposed innovation with suspicion and resistance almost regardless of the circumstances.

The antismoking campaign, for example, amounted to a test of physician response to the notion of pharmacies operating in a counseling role. To the Association's disappointment, though to no one's great surprise, the doctors viewed the program as an incursion on their own professional territory. They applied pressure and got the courses taken off the market.

Similarly, the pharmacists found little demand for their home health care packages for newly discharged patients, partly because hospitals and the public health-insurance agency viewed the pharmacies as competitors and declined to recommend the service.

Self-care packages also fared poorly. True, on Blood Pressure Day in 1991, thousands of Danes came to pharmacies all over the country for blood pressure and cholesterol readings, but as a general rule, people wanted their physicians to go on conducting even simple tests and recommending even basic treatments free of charge, the way they had always done in the past.

Clearly, the pharmacies were doing something wrong, and it wasn't hard to figure out what. The new strategy itself was a good one as far as it went—reinvention of a centuries-old business to fit new social and commercial realities, development of denser offerings, more interaction with suppliers and customers to co-produce value. The problem was credibility.

Rethinking Business Alliances

Denmark's individual pharmacies had always been private businesses, and their professional Association had always been a nonprofit organization. But in recent years, the Association had strayed further and further into outright commercial competition. With their customers, the pharmacists still had a reputation for professionalism and excellence. Within its industry, the Association was developing a reputation for sharp elbows.

The Association urgently needed to improve its relations with the political system and other stakeholders in the health care sector. To achieve this end, it had to behave a little less like a competitor and think more seriously and consistently about the co-productive constellations in which it wished to operate. It needed to rethink its concept of reconfiguration and push its new strategy further.

The Association is a purely voluntary organization of independent pharmacists. It has long had the authority to negotiate drug prices with the government, but it has never had the power to force its strategic thinking on individual member pharmacies. Yet the process of business reconfiguration is in great part a process of building new competencies. The government may have moved slowly on deregulation, but the pharmacies had also moved slowly in learning to understand their new roles in the health care complex.

In 1969, the Association had established an educational center outside Copenhagen to centralize the training of licensed pharmacy technicians and to offer its pharmacist members continuing, postgraduate education in new pharmaceutical developments. In the 1980s, as the Association's new direction began to take hold, the school broadened its program to include courses in marketing, service management, customer orientation, and business skills. Now the old center also became a tool for promoting ideas and disseminating the Association's new understanding of its business.

In 1990, to eliminate once and for all its direct competition with the drug companies, the Association sold its drug manufacturing subsidiary and withdrew from pharmaceutical production for the first time in its history.

In 1991, the Association further redesigned its organization and divided its activities in two. It assembled its business assets—computer operations, wholesaling, and the profits from the sale of its drug-production subsidiary—into a separate company that operated according to normal business principles. Strategic planning and coordination of educational, informational, and social services remained not-for-profit activities and stayed in the hands of the Association itself, strongly backed by profits from business activities.

The Association also increased its past efforts to build alliances with Denmark's national organizations for the elderly and disabled, as well as those for heart disease, epilepsy, asthma, and diabetes, among others. The Association now also works closely with the Danish Consumer Council in areas such as drug information and labeling.

The Association's progressive efforts at health care-sector redesign won it international acclaim, and this exposure helped it to forge alliances with sister organizations across Europe and around the world. In 1985, the Association urged the World Health Organization to work more closely with pharmacists, and this led to the establishment of the Europharm Forum, linking pharmaceutical organizations in WHO's European region. In 1988, WHO issued guidelines recommending that pharmacists assume a central role in health care systems as drug advisors par excellence to patients, physicians, and other professionals.

Perhaps most important of all, the Association is now taking part in an international, multicenter study of the pharmacist's role in drug therapies. In Denmark, the research project is working with 300 asthma patients in a double-blind study of pharmacist-assisted asthma therapies. Because the study incorporates a new division of responsibility among patient, physician, and pharmacist, the Association has named two doctors—a professor of medicine and a clinical pharmacologist—to the project's steering committee.

The result of these efforts has been striking. In 1992, the Association reintroduced its antismoking courses in a joint venture with Europharm Forum and WHO. This time, thanks to the Association's alliances and its international standing, Danish physicians found themselves in de facto recognition of the pharmacies' counseling activities. The program was a box-office success, and WHO wants to export it to other parts of Europe.

Also in 1992, the Association's business subsidiary acquired 10% of Denmark's only ambulance operator, creating a co-productive alliance between two businesses with the same set of customers. Among other things, this alliance has revived the home-care concept with a system for dependable delivery of drug, support, and security services to the elderly and to patients recently discharged from the hospital.

Overall, greater efficiency has allowed the pharmacies to increase their net profits steadily while reducing gross profits substantially, a strong argument for preserving their retail monopoly. Moreover, the Association, while one of the world's smallest, is economically one of the world's strongest, with more than $200 million in assets, not, of course, counting the value of the independent pharmacies themselves. In 1992, the Association developed a plan that pushes reconfiguration and co-production into the twenty-first century with new initiatives that saved Danish taxpayers more than $16 million the first year.

The pharmacies' struggles are no doubt far from over. Their business environment is also a political environment, a fact that has complicated their efforts to work with other health care players to produce new offerings and enlarge the opportunities for value creation available to the average citizen-customer. Yet what the pharmacies discovered was that reconfiguration made more than political sense. It also made business sense. The reinvention of any business constellation is at least partly a matter of thinking through the social implications of change. In the end, new offerings have gradually allowed the pharmacies to get a far higher return on their knowledge base and their customer base than they ever enjoyed in the past.

Increasingly, the companies that survive and thrive are those that look beyond their immediate boundaries to the social and business systems in which they are enmeshed and discover new ways to reconfigure those systems in order to reinvent value for their customers.

French Concessions: Of Customers and Competencies

In an economy founded on the new logic of value, only two assets really matter: knowledge and relationships or a company's competencies and its customers. Competencies are the technologies, specialized expertise, business processes and techniques that a company has accumulated over time and packaged in its offerings. But knowledge alone is not enough. Obviously, a company's competencies are worthless without customers willing to pay for them. Thus the other key asset for any company is its established customer base.

A company's relationship with a customer is really an access channel to the customer's ongoing value-creating activities. Any customer, whether another business or an individual, uses a wide range of inputs in order to create value. A company's offerings have value to the degree that customers can use them as inputs to leverage their own value creation. In this respect, then, companies don't profit from customers. They profit from customers' value-creating activities.

One of the chief strategic challenges of the new economy is to integrate knowledge and relationships—devise a good fit between competencies and customers and keep that fit current. In order to exploit established relationships, in other words, a company needs to enlarge its knowledge base continuously. It must invest in an ever-broadening range of knowledge resources and combine ever-expanding kinds of knowledge into its offerings.

What is more, these investments in new knowledge can become so large that a company's own offerings to its existing customer base are no longer adequate to recoup its investment. So the new knowledge tends to propel companies into new businesses in search of new relationships with new customers. And the cycle repeats.

For an example of how this dialogue between competencies and customers, knowledge and relationships, is shaping the nature of business competition, consider the recent evolution of two French corporations: Compagnie Générale des Eaux and Lyonnaise des Eaux Dumez. With 1992 revenues of $27 billion and $18 billion respectively, Générale and Lyonnaise rank 6th and 11th among France's largest companies. They are also among that country's most technologically dynamic and successful global competitors.

As their names suggest, Générale des Eaux and Lyonnaise des Eaux Dumez got their start by providing water to French cities and towns, and they are still very much in the water business. Between them, Générale and Lyonnaise provide drinking water to about 37 million French residents. In addition, Lyonnaise is now the biggest private water company in the world, with some 35 or 40 million consumers on 6 continents. Générale is the next largest. But to think of either as a water company entirely fails to capture the complexity and dynamism of their business or, for that matter, its fundamental logic.

In addition to water, Générale and Lyonnaise and their numerous subsidiaries provide cities and towns with everything from heating systems, sewers, and utilities to hazardous waste treatment, municipal construction, nursing homes, golf courses, and even funeral services. In Toulouse, for example, Générale not only manages the city's water distribution but has also developed a local recreation center known as Aqualand and is an investor in the city's cable television network. In Avignon, Lyonnaise manages the city's historical monuments, art museum, public gardens, and parks. And a Lyonnaise subsidiary, Pompes Funébres Générales, is the world's largest undertaker, handling almost 40% of all funerals in France. Some of these businesses seem to follow logically from the business of water delivery, others seem to represent an aggressive effort at diversification. But, in fact, all these activities grow organically from a particularly French understanding of the business that Générale and Lyonnaise are in and of the special skills that they possess.

In most Western countries, public infrastructure is a public responsibility. City (or state or county) governments put out tenders for public-works projects to be built according to designs and specifications supplied by the city or its consultants and paid for using its authority to issue bonds and assume debt. Construction is carried out under contract with the city; operation and maintenance of the completed system is done by the city or contracted out, often piecemeal and for brief periods. From beginning to end, the brains controlling the project are on the city payroll or work for the city as consultants. This tender system is nearly universal in the Anglo-Saxon world and is standard practice in most of Europe as well.

But the French handle these matters differently. Since the nineteenth century, France has actively encouraged a separation between the political responsibility and the production responsibility for public services. While elected officials must answer to the voters for the provision of roads, utilities, and other amenities, and while water assets, for example, are publicly owned, private companies act as *concessionaires*, designing the projects and specifications, raising the capital, building the infrastructure, managing the assets, bearing the risks, pocketing the profits, and assuming a large part of the local government's relevant authority and responsibility in order to do so. In effect, the government—local or national—delegates virtually all its public-service duties and prerogatives to a private company, retaining only the political responsibility for governance. The social reasoning behind this separation of responsibilities is essentially twofold.

First, concessions have allowed an activist French state to finance extensive infrastructure development without using the public purse. Government simply delegated the obligation to build and paid for it with the right to operate. The first such concessions were granted by France's strong central government in the nineteenth century for the construction of canals. (See "French Concessions" at the end of this article for a brief account of their history.) Later, the state gave concessions for aqueducts, water distribution systems, market halls, and railways. Later still, concessions were used to construct gas and electrical networks and tramways. The concessionaire designed, built, and paid for these systems. The government owned them and granted a concession on their profitable operation for periods of 30 years or more.

Second, concessions have kept governments out of the commercial, industrial sphere and helped to protect them from spiraling debt and operational waste. Moreover, by tying profit to the efficient operation of the assets once installed, the concession system also made good use of the capitalist interests that sought to profit from public infrastructure construction. Until well into the twentieth century, French courts typically disallowed the efforts of cities to create municipal companies and operate public services for themselves.

But perhaps the concession system's most profound effect has been on the concessionaires themselves: on the way they developed and how they now view their competencies and their business strategies. There is a French term that managers at both Générale and Lyonnaise use to describe their distinctive expertise: *aménageur des villes*, roughly translated "urban-systems designer and outfitter." Put simply, the business of Générale and Lyonnaise is not any one service so much as the production of entire systems of services, and their core competence is not water or even utilities but rather the financial, social, legal, managerial, and technical engineering that ensures the smooth operation of public service infrastructures.

Developing Knowledge for Relationships

For French concessionaires, the principal business risk has never been the ordinary hazards of the marketplace: day-to-day competition, fluctuating demand, changing fashion. The great challenge (in addition to getting the concession renewed for another 30 or 40 years) has always been to find new services to offer an existing customer base and so to exploit further the concessionaire's own investment in knowledge and knowledge workers. Générale and Lyonnaise have addressed this problem by developing a higher order interorganizational competence: their expertise is precisely that of developing, acquiring, and integrating a broad cross-section of technologies and knowledge and focusing them on their customers' continuously evolving value creation.

Générale has some 2,000 subsidiaries and Lyonnaise about 720, ranging in size from very small to very large and grouped according to specialization or *métier*. Both Générale and Lyonnaise see themselves as necessarily multilocal companies, and their subsidiaries enjoy considerable autonomy. At the same time, both companies concentrate intently on the possibilities for synergy and on the management of integration. Générale's 60 *métiers*, for example, are richly interconnected at every level and within every jurisdiction in

If no Générale company can produce what the client wants, then Générale will create a company that can.

order to help services build on each other and to open the door to new services as soon as, and sometimes before, the client sees a need for them. This continuous, ad hoc flowering of co-productive relationships among subsidiaries and between subsidiaries and clients represents an ongoing reinvention of the parent company. As one Générale executive told us, "Our people have no a priori right to say no to a client request. If one of the companies in our group cannot produce what the client wants, then we will create a company that can."

Générale and Lyonnaise have put France on the cutting edge of R&D on water purification, transport, and waste-water treatment. In Méry-sur-Oise, Générale has established the first chlorine-free water-treatment system in the world. In Tokyo, Lyonnaise researchers are working with the Japanese to develop compact water-purification plants using biological systems.

The companies have also become leaders in emerging markets for "green" industrial services, such as waste management, a market estimated at $34.5 billion in Europe alone in 1991 and expected to double by the year 2000. A Générale subsidiary runs Europe's largest hazardous-waste-treatment facility in Limay, outside Paris.

Finally, the two companies have also emphasized the technological synergies that integration can provide. In Paris, for example, they use the garbage and trash their street-cleaning subsidiaries collect to fuel cogeneration plants. Ten percent of Parisians heat their homes with electricity produced by garbage incineration.

As Générale and Lyonnaise invest in a broader and broader range of technologies and expertise, they seek out new customers in order to defray the costs of the investments. One way is to provide similar services to customers in the private sector. Both companies are now managing outsourced services for private companies, for example, hazardous waste disposal.

Even more important, as city services around the world become privatized, both companies are moving aggressively to compete on a global scale. Lyonnaise has built and managed water distribution networks in more than 50 cities on 6 continents. Over the last four years, Générale has developed a $60 million business managing waste-water-treatment plants and drinking-water-production facilities for small towns in the United States.

What's more, the companies' integrated solutions are proving to be a strong competitive advantage. In contrast to companies that specialize in only one aspect of public-infrastructure provision—such as Bechtel in engineering, Veba in energy systems, or Browning-Ferris Industries in waste management—Générale and Lyonnaise can provide cities and towns with an integrated package of offerings. The advantage for the client is that some activities—for example, cable television or hazardous-waste management—can take years to become profitable. The city cannot afford to take on the development expense itself, and a tender for this kind of infrastructure must take into account several years of operating losses. But long-term investments of precisely this kind are the stock-in-trade of concessionaires like Générale and Lyonnaise, which see such investments in the larger context of competence and customer development.

Public service packages that expand from one expertise to another have thus become not only a strong source of profit growth but also a powerful negotiating card in dealing with local governments. In the city of Macao, for example, Lyonnaise first won a contract for water distribution and waste-water treatment from the Portuguese colonial authorities. Then the company used its presence in the local market to acquire a concession for the generation and distribution of electricity. This in turn led to construction of a new electric power station, while the water concession led to the establishment in Macao of the largest water-analysis laboratory in Asia.

So far, Générale and Lyonnaise have tried to manage the interplay of competencies and customers under a single corporate umbrella: by creating new companies or acquiring existing ones and integrating them into the group. A complementary tactic, of course, is to form partnerships with outside companies that have developed different sets of resources. Such alliances permit the concessionaire to provide its traditional customer base with appropriately denser offerings without the expense of developing new expertise of its own. Moreover, alliances also provide conduits to new customer bases and allow companies to capitalize on their core knowledge by selling it to the customers of their allies.

Trends appear to be pushing Générale and Lyonnaise in this direction. Générale, for example, has formed alliances with several other European companies that are, in the words of one Générale executive, "clients as well as suppliers." For that matter, Générale and Lyonnaise themselves, while relentless competitors at home, have in a few cases bid jointly on contracts to provide drinking water and waste-water treatment in other parts of the world.

However it takes place, the integration of different disciplines into viable global offerings is a skill that Générale and Lyonnaise have raised to the level of a virtual *metacompetence*. They have not merely learned to combine expertise in construction, engineering, finance, operational management, project management, risk management, infrastructure

The secret of value creation is building a better and better fit between relationships and knowledge.

development, contractual law, social policy, and much more, they have made consistent use of the logic of public responsibility—their clients' logic—to leverage this bundle of value-creating activities.

The concession system is still unique to France, where it is regarded as unexportable, perhaps even untranslatable. Yet its obvious benefits to the taxpayer and its clear advantages for the quality of infrastructure construction and operation have made it an object of study around the world, and new jurisdictions are adapting it to fit new circumstances. The regulatory bodies of the EEC are giving the concession system particular scrutiny.

Regardless of its future, however, the concession system has already made hugely creative demands on concessionaires by requiring strategic skill on three levels: Concessionaires have learned to master the design and management of interconnected, co-productive offerings. They have learned how to mobilize value creation in their customers and partners by reconfiguring roles, relationships, and structures. And they have learned the art of perpetually reinventing value in a dialogue between competencies and customers. These are the skills that have kept concessionaires alive and profitable for more than one hundred years. And these are the skills that winning corporations will have to acquire in the post-assembly-line economy that is now emerging.

French Concessions

FROM THE VERY BEGINNING, concessionaires took a broad view of their business. Napoleon III created Compagnie Générale des Eaux by imperial decree in 1853, and the Rothschilds bought 5,000 of its 80,000 shares, becoming the company's banker. Générale won a 99-year water-distribution concession from Lyons that same year, added Nantes in 1854, expanded steadily into smaller communities, entered a complex agreement with the city of Paris in the early 1860s, began introducing new technologies in the 1890s aimed at the improvement of water quality as well as quantity, and eventually moved into heating, construction, and other services.

It was Crédit Lyonnaise that founded Lyonnaise des Eaux in 1880 to operate water and lighting systems in Cannes. In 1891, Lyonnaise created its first subsidiary to build and operate a sewer system in Marseilles. Throughout the remainder of the nineteenth century and through the first half of the twentieth, Lyonnaise engaged heavily in various types of infrastructure construction and operation, all of it by concession. By the late 1930s, Lyonnaise was preeminent in the operation of gas and electrical networks throughout France.

Although privately owned concessionaires provided the vast majority of public services in France by 1900, the concession system suffered a series of setbacks in the first half of the twentieth century. The first blow came in 1916, when municipalities were made liable for the unpaid debts of their concessionaires, and the second in 1926, when cities and towns were finally granted the right to own and operate their own public-service companies. As municipal companies began to replace local concessionaires, the great national concessions also began to vanish: the airlines in 1933, the railways in 1937. By 1939, concessionaires operated less than half of French public services, and in 1946, a wave of nationalizations stripped them of much of what remained, including most of the French electrical grid.

Then in 1951, public-service policy did another about face as the need to rebuild infrastructure, neglected during and after the war, once again far outstripped the taxpayers' capacity to foot the bill. The law was altered, concessions made a wholesale comeback, and concessionaires like Générale and Lyonnaise regained their raison d'être and their former expansive energy.

Today concessionaires—some of them partly controlled by state-owned institutional investors—operate not only the majority of public utilities in France but also toll motorways, bridges, marinas, ports, parking lots, hospitals, housing developments, and soon, perhaps, prisons.

Originally published in July–August 1993
Reprint 93408

From Lean Production to the Lean Enterprise

JAMES P. WOMACK AND
DANIEL T. JONES

Executive Summary

SINCE THE PUBLICATION OF their 1991 book about lean production in the auto industry, *The Machine That Changed the World,* James Womack and Daniel Jones have seen North American and European companies make amazing improvements by implementing lean-production techniques. The authors have realized that linking these individual breakthroughs up and down the value chain, creating a *lean enterprise,* is the next step in achieving superior performance.

The lean enterprise is a group of individuals, functions, and legally separate but operationally synchronized companies that creates, sells, and services a family of products. Few companies have created a lean enterprise, and understandably. Individuals, functions, and companies have needs that conflict with each other and with those of the lean enterprise. The strengths and weaknesses of the German, U.S., and Japanese industrial traditions suggest that trade-offs between these three entities are inevitable.

Womack and Jones believe, however, that the lean enterprise can satisfy these conflicting needs if managers offer career paths that alternate between concentration on a value chain and knowledge building within functions; turn functions into schools; focus companies on a narrower set of tasks; and implement a new code of behavior to overcome the Cold War relations that prevail among companies in most value chains today.

A concerted effort by companies across the industrial landscape to embrace the lean enterprise and find new tasks for excess employees will be superior to any industrial policy that a government could devise.

IN OUR BOOK *The Machine That Changed the World,* we explained how companies can dramatically improve their performance by embracing the "lean production" approach pioneered by Toyota. By eliminating unnecessary steps, aligning all steps in an activity in a continuous flow, recombining labor into cross-functional teams dedicated to that activity, and continually striving for improvement, companies can develop, produce, and distribute products with *half or less* of the human effort, space, tools, time, and overall expense. They can also become vastly more flexible and responsive to customer desires.

Over the past three years, we have helped a variety of North American and European companies implement lean-production techniques and have studied many others that have adopted the approach. We've seen numerous examples of amazing improvements in a *specific* activity in a *single* company. But these experiences have also made us realize that applying lean techniques to discrete activities is not the end of the road. If individual breakthroughs can be linked up and down the value chain to form a continuous *value stream* that creates, sells, and services a family of products, the performance of the whole can be raised to a dramatically higher level. We think that value-creating activities can be joined, but this effort will require a new organizational model: the *lean enterprise.*

As we envision it, the lean enterprise is a group of individuals, functions, and legally separate but operationally synchronized companies. The notion of the value stream defines the lean enterprise. The group's mission is collectively to analyze and focus a value stream so that it does everything involved in supplying a good or service (from development and production to sales and maintenance) in a way that provides maximum value to the customer. The lean enterprise differs dramatically from the much-discussed "virtual corporation," whose members are constantly coming and going. There is no way that such an unstable entity can sustain the collaboration needed to apply lean techniques along an entire value stream.

We do not know of any group of companies that has yet created a lean enterprise, and understandably. Doing so will entail radical changes in employment policies, the role of functions within companies, and the relationships among the companies of a value stream. Managers will have to concentrate on the performance of the enterprise rather than on the performance of individual people, functions, and companies. This is especially important because even though one company will be the "team leader," the enterprise must be unified by shared logic and shared pains and gains.

Admittedly, linking lean activities is difficult. We've been struck repeatedly by how hard it is for managers, accustomed to overseeing discrete functions and narrow activities while looking out for the interests of their own companies, even to see the entire value stream. Why should companies set their sights on the lean enterprise when so many are still struggling to master lean production?

Any manager aspiring to a lean enterprise must understand the conflicting needs of individuals, functions, and companies.

Because unless all members of a value stream pull together, it may be impossible for any one member to maintain momentum. (See "Lucas: Undermined from Without and Within" at the end of this article.) Even if one member makes a lot of progress in becoming lean, neither that member nor the stream as a whole will reap the full benefits if another member falls short.

The Three Needs

Getting managers to think in terms of the value stream is the critical first step to achieving a lean enterprise. Managers who have taken this first step, however, have often run into stiff resistance from employees and functional units as well as from other companies in the stream. Individuals, functions, and companies have legitimate needs that conflict with those of the value stream. Anyone aspiring to a lean enterprise must first understand these needs and how to satisfy them. (See "Chrysler's Next Challenge: Building Lean Enterprises") at the end of this article.

NEEDS OF THE INDIVIDUAL

For most people, having a job is the minimum requirement for self-respect and financial well-being. Thus it is ludicrous to assume that people will identify and orchestrate changes that eliminate their jobs. Because making any process lean immediately creates large numbers of excess workers and then continually reduces the amount of effort needed, the jobs problem is a major obstacle confronting any enterprise that is trying to make a performance leap and then sustain its momentum.

Beyond a job, most of us need a career to give us a sense that we are developing our abilities and are "going somewhere." Also, most of us need a "home" that defines who we are in our work lives. These yearnings can be filled by a function ("I'm an electrical engineer"), by a company ("I'm a Matsushita employee"), or even by a union ("I'm a Steelworker"). But the value stream itself cannot fill these needs for long. While functions and companies endure, an employee's position within a specific value stream is tied to the life of the product.

NEEDS OF FUNCTIONS

In order to use and expand the knowledge of employees, companies must organize this knowledge into functions, such as engineering, marketing, purchasing, accounting, and quality assurance. But functions do much more than accumulate knowledge; they teach that knowledge to those who identify their careers with the function, and they search continually for new knowledge. In the so-called learning organization, functions are where learning is collected, systematized, and deployed. Functions, therefore, need a secure place in any organization.

Because of the required depth of knowledge, the time and effort needed to obtain that knowledge, and its inherent portability (much knowledge can be carried from one employer to another), functional specialists often feel a stronger commitment to their function and its intellectual tradition than they do to either the value stream or the company. But focusing processes, which is the means of making organizations lean, requires a high degree of cross-functional cooperation. It is not surprising, then, that many executives these days view their functions as obstacles.

Some executives and business theorists advocate permanently assigning members of functions to multifunctional teams as the solution to this conflict between function and process. Others propose weakening functions or subsuming the activities of "minor" functions like marketing within product teams. Both solutions may work for a while but will weaken companies in the long run.

NEEDS OF COMPANIES

The narrower the scope of responsibility, the more easily a company can calculate costs and the benefits it generates and see the results of its improvement efforts. Therefore, the value stream should be segmented so that each company is responsible for a narrow set of activities.

Throughout most of industrial history, the value chain has usually been integrated vertically within one company, or one company has dominated the other companies making up the chain. These practices make sense; after all, a company's most basic need is to survive by making an adequate return, and weak links in the chain can be a far greater threat to a company's survival than the vagaries of the end-user market. As a result, companies understandably consider control more important than efficiency or responsiveness. The natural response during hard times is for the strongest company to reintegrate as many activities as it can within its corporate walls or for each company in the value chain to grab as much of the profits or revenues as it can from its neighbors.

Hints from Three Industrial Traditions

Given all these conflicting needs, it is easy to see why few enterprises achieve maximum efficiency, flexibility, and customer responsiveness. Nor is blasting clear the channel—the stated mission of the process-reengineering movement—likely to provide relief for more than a short spell before the conflicting needs of individuals, functions, and companies gum things up again.

In searching for a solution, it's useful to look anew at the three preeminent industrial traditions: the German, the American, and the Japanese. Each has derived different strengths by trying to satisfy the needs of either the function, the individual, or the company. The conventional wisdom has been that the three traditions, whose shortcomings are the product of these unavoidable trade-offs, are mutually exclusive. We disagree. In the course of our extensive research on German, U.S., and Japanese companies, it has occurred to us that there is a fourth approach. We believe that our model of the lean enterprise will satisfy the needs of individuals, functions, *and* companies. The end result will offer greater value to the customer than the existing traditions can.

THE GERMAN TRADITION

The backbone of German industry has been its intense focus on deep technical knowledge organized into rigidly defined functions. Individuals progress in their careers by climbing the functional ladder. And companies strive to defend their positions in a value chain by hoarding proprietary knowledge within their technical functions.

The consequence of this focus has been great technical depth and an ability to compete globally by offering customized products with superior performance. The weakness of the German tradition, strikingly apparent in the 1990s, is its hostility to cross-functional cooperation. Mercedes-Benz, for example, requires three times the number of hours Toyota requires to engineer and manufacture a comparable luxury car, largely because the engineering functions won't talk to each other. Mercedes makes durable, high-performance cars, but with too many labor-intensive loops in the development process and too little attention to manufacturability. The same holds true for almost all German industries, which have discovered that the world will no longer buy enough customized goods at the high prices required to support the system's inherent inefficiency.

THE AMERICAN TRADITION

The individual has always been at the center of U.S. society. At the beginning of this century, the lack of strong functional and craft traditions and the willingness of suppliers to collaborate with assemblers were major advantages in introducing continuous flow and mass production.

But extreme individualism created its own needs. In the postwar era, managers sought portable professional credentials (e.g., an MBA) and generic expertise independent of a particular business (e.g., finance). And rather than stressing cooperation, each company in a value chain, itself acting as an individual, sought to create its own defendable turf.

The consequence was that U.S. industry gradually became as functional as German industry, but self-preservation, rather than a desire for technical knowledge, drove functionalism in the United States. At the same time, the "every company for itself" tendency most evident in hard times greatly reduced the ability of U.S. companies to think together about the entire value stream. Even though the willingness of Americans to innovate by breaking away from employers and traditional intercompany relationships imparts a real advantage today in nascent industries like information processing and biotechnology, this extreme individualism has caused the United States to lose its lead in efficient production.

The cult of the individual has undermined the United States's position as the world's most efficient manufacturer.

THE JAPANESE TRADITION

The Japanese have stressed the needs of the company, which is hardly surprising given the centuries-old feudal tradition of obligation between companies and employees and between big companies and their smaller suppliers and distributors. Government policy, with its focus on production rather than individual consumption, has reinforced this emphasis. The enormous benefit of the Japanese tradition has been the ability of big companies to focus on the needs of the entire value stream unimpeded by functional fiefdoms, career paths within functions, and the constant struggles between members of the value stream to gain an advantage over each other.

But such an exclusive focus on the company produces corresponding weaknesses, which have become apparent over time. For example, the technical functions are weak in most Japanese companies despite the overwhelming dominance of engineers in management. Because most engineers have spent practically all their careers on cross-functional teams developing products or improving production processes, they have gotten better and better at applying what they already know. But the creation of new knowledge back in the technical functions has languished. As a result, many Japanese companies (from Toyota in cars to Matsushita in consumer electronics) that prospered by commercializing and incrementally improving well-understood product and process technologies have now largely cleared the shelf of available ideas for generating fundamentally new, innovative products and processes.

Sony is a case in point. The company recently acknowledged that, for the first time in its history, no dramatic product breakthroughs were imminent and that it would try to defend its competitive position by adopting lean techniques to cut costs in its increasingly mature product lines. We applaud, of course, whenever a company adopts lean techniques. However, these should complement rather than substitute for innovation. Sony must address the weakness of its core technical functions in addition to becoming lean.

Another weakness inherent in the Japanese system is that preserving feudal relationships has become more important than responding to shifts in the market. During the last five years, Japanese companies with massive export surpluses should have redeployed production so that their output in a given region corresponded more closely to sales in that region. Instead, constraints on reassigning employees to new enterprises and abandoning traditional second- and third-tier suppliers caused many big companies to invest in additional domestic capacity for making the same families of products. This is why so many companies, including the model company Toyota, found themselves in deep trouble when the yen strengthened.

New Models for Careers, Functions, and the Company

The critical challenge for managers today is to synchronize the needs of the individual, the function, the company, and the value stream in a way that will yield the full benefits of the lean enterprise while actually increasing individual opportunities, functional strength, and the well-being of member companies. Achieving this balance will require new management techniques, organizational forms, and principles of shared endeavor.

ALTERNATING CAREER PATHS

If we have learned anything in recent years about the value stream, it is that individuals must be totally dedicated to a specific process for the value stream to flow smoothly and efficiently. The old division of labor, which shuttled the product from department to department, must give way to a recombination of labor so that fewer workers, organized in focused teams, can expedite the value flow without bottlenecks or queues. Similarly, functional specialists involved in product development must completely focus on their task in a team context.

But there is a problem. The individual facing permanent assignment to a cross-functional team is being asked to abandon his or her functional career path. At the same time, key functions face the loss of power and importance. When both individuals and functions feel threatened by streamlined processes, these processes won't be streamlined for very long.

The solution is a career path that alternates between concentration on a specific value stream (a family of products) and dedicated, intense knowledge building within functions. These functions must include a new process-management function (in place of industrial engineering and quality assurance) that instills a process perspective in everyone from the top to the bottom of the company.

In following this new career path, the individual's know-how will still be growing. But the value stream itself will get his or her undivided attention for extended periods. Making this model work will be the primary task of the human resource function, which is responsible for ensuring that each individual has a coherent career—a key to attracting and retaining employees.

The concept of an alternating career path has nothing to do with matrix organizations, in which everyone has two bosses. In this new model, the process leader rates an individual's performance while an individual is dedicated to a process, but the function head rates performance while the individual is back in the function. The career planner in human resources, the function head, and the process leader decide jointly where the individual should go next.

Honda has embraced this approach in Japan and North America, particularly for engineers. When engineers join Honda, they go through a rotation, common in Japanese companies, that begins with several months on a production line, followed by short stints in marketing, product planning, and sales. Honda's practice then diverges from the Japanese norm of assigning engineers to and keeping them in process teams. At Honda, the young engineer's first extended assignment is on a product-development team, where he or she performs routine engineering calculations. This assignment continues for the life of the development activity, or up to three years.

When individuals and functions feel threatened by streamlined processes, these processes won't be streamlined for long.

After this job, the young engineer is assigned to his or her technical specialty within the engineering department to begin a skills-upgrading process. As part of this phase, the individual is assigned to an advanced engineering effort involving a search for new techniques or capabilities that the company wants to master. The engineer is then typically reassigned to a development team for a new product to perform more complex engineering tasks that call on his or her newly acquired knowledge. After this development effort, the engineer goes back to the "home" engineering function to begin another learn-apply-learn cycle.

FUNCTIONS BECOME SCHOOLS

The problem with functions in most companies today is that they perform the wrong tasks. Purchasing should not purchase. Engineering should not engineer. Production should not produce. In the lean enterprise, functions have two major roles. The first is to serve as a school. They should systematically summarize current knowledge, search for new knowledge, and teach all this to their members, who then spend time on value-creating process teams. (See "Unipart: Turning Functions into Schools" at the end of this article.)

The second role of functions is to develop guidelines—the best practices—for, say, purchasing or marketing and to draw up a roster of those companies eligible to be long-term partners in the value stream (suppliers, in the case of the purchasing department). With their counterparts in companies up and down the value stream, functions should also develop rules for governing how they will work together to solve problems that span the companies and for establishing behavioral codes so that one company does not exploit another.

So who actually performs the tasks that these functions traditionally handled? Cross-functional product-development and production teams should select suppliers, develop products, and oversee routine production activities. The traditional purchasing department, for example, should define the principles of enduring relationships with suppliers, draw up the roster of eligible suppliers, and strive to improve continuously the performance of every sup-

Nissan's British subsidiary turned its worst suppliers into its best by helping them improve their key processes.

plier. The product-development team should perform the purchasing department's traditional job of deciding to obtain a specific amount of a specific item at a target price from a specific supplier for the life of the product.

The experience of Nissan's British subsidiary provides a striking example of what can happen when a purchasing department rethinks its mission. Nissan had serious problems during the 1989 production launch of the Primera, its first car designed for the European market, when several suppliers disrupted production by failing to deliver workable parts on time. The normal course of action in Britain would have been to replace the miscreants. Instead, Nissan's British purchasing department teamed up with the Nissan R&D center to place supplier-development teams of Nissan engineers inside each supplier for extended periods to improve their key processes. Nissan's theory was that setting high standards and giving the suppliers advice on how to meet them would produce superior results. Two years later, when Nissan began production of the Micra, a new small car, this approach had transformed these suppliers from the Nissan subsidiary's worst into its best.

What is the role of other functions? Marketing defines principles of enduring relationships with customers and/or distributors and identifies suitable partners. The traditional marketing and sales tasks of specifying the product, taking orders, and scheduling delivery become the work of the product-development and production teams. Engineering defines the best engineering practices, which it teaches to engineers. It also searches for new capabilities, such as new materials to reduce weight in its products. By undertaking such jobs, the engineering function extends the expertise of the discipline by finding ways to overcome the shortcomings of today's products and processes. It can then apply its new knowledge to the next generation of products or to entirely new products. The product-development team performs all routine engineering; it solves problems that have been solved before for similar products.

Finally, a new process-management function (which still does not exist in the vast majority of companies) does three things: it defines the rules for managing cross-functional teams and the continuous flow of production, including quality assurance; it teaches team leaders in product development and production how to apply these rules; and it constantly searches for better approaches. The old departmental structures within production—molding, painting, assembly, quality assurance—disappear into the continuous-flow production teams in charge of making families of products.

While functions become "support" for value-creating process teams, every function paradoxically has a deeper and more coherent knowledge base than was possible when it divided its attention between thinking and doing. Moreover, this knowledge base is more relevant to the company's long-term needs because function members returning from value-creating assignments in the processes bring new questions for the function to answer. Constantly applying knowledge in this way fights the tendency of all intellectual activities to veer off into abstractions when left in isolation.

A SHARPER FOCUS FOR COMPANIES

Most companies today do too much and do much of it poorly. In the world of the lean enterprise, each company in a value stream will tackle a narrower set of tasks that it can do well.

The company that is the assembler, for example, may find that it no longer needs to design or produce any of the major component systems in its product because product development (in collaboration with suppliers and distributors) and final assembly are its real skills. The component-system supplier may discover it no longer needs to make the parts in its systems because design of the complete system (in collaboration with customers and its own suppliers) is its competitive advantage. New companies may emerge to design component systems or make discrete parts and to supply services, like cleaning facilities, that are tangential to the mission of focused companies. Japanese industries, whose companies have been less vertically integrated than U.S. and European companies, have long taken this approach, and many North American and European industries, from aerospace to automotive to appliances, are following suit.

At the same time, all companies will need to participate in several enterprises involving different sets of companies in order to obtain the stability that any one value stream, with its inevitable ups and downs, cannot provide. Stability aside, companies will want to participate in a range of streams involving a range of products or services in order to learn from companies that think in different ways. This is a key to continuous improvement.

A New Code of Behavior

For lean companies to be able to work together and to be assured of survival, they must develop new principles for regulating their behavior. Cold War–like relations prevail among companies in most value chains today. No one would suggest that the real Cold War would have been resolved if the Eastern and Western blocs simply trusted each other. The current notion that companies can end their hostilities simply by embracing trust is equally implausible.

All negotiated peace arrangements, including those in the corporate world, entail an agreement on the principles of just behavior and procedures that enable each party to verify that others are keeping their end of the deal. When this latter condition is met, trust occurs naturally because everyone can see what's going on.

Achieving cooperation within the value stream is particularly difficult. Every stream needs a "team leader," a company that orchestrates the decision to form an enterprise, pulls together the full complement of member companies, and leads the joint analysis of the total enterprise stream. Unfortunately, industrial history is replete

An enterprise must draw up a code of behavior to keep its members in line.

with stories of companies that have used their leadership positions to extract advantage from upstream and downstream partners. And the overwhelming expectation is that these leaders will continue to behave this way.

Obviously, the principles for regulating behavior within a value stream will vary with the nature of the product and the degree of familiarity of its member companies. However, there must be clear agreements on target costing (deciding what price the customer would pay for a product and then working backward to determine how that product can be made so that it also delivers a profit), acceptable levels of process performance, the rate of continuous improvement (and cost reductions), consistent accounting systems to analyze costs, and formulas for splitting pain and gain.

In every case, companies in a stream must discuss the total activity, the performance requirements for individual activities, the verification procedures for performance, and the reward formulas. They must do this before they embark on the task and adopt explicit principles of interaction that everyone agrees are just. This is what Nissan is attempting to do.

When Nissan established its manufacturing operation in Britain in 1986, it could not bring most of its suppliers from Japan. (Its production volume was initially too small, and it had agreed to make cars with a high level of local content in return for start-up aid from the British government.) But the European companies that were chosen as suppliers were initially unsure of the depth of Nissan's commitment to them. Would Nissan eventually replace them with members of its own *keiretsu* from Japan? Would the company's commitment to its European suppliers survive the next economic downturn?

To dispel these doubts, Nissan has worked hard to establish and adhere to principles governing its relationships with suppliers. These include a permanent commitment to suppliers that make a continuous effort to improve; a clear role for each supplier within the supply chain; a joint examination of ways the entire value stream can reduce costs; and a commitment to help improve processes when problems emerge. These principles explain Nissan's decision to help inept suppliers improve rather than dumping them, a decision that sent a powerful signal to the rest of its suppliers and strengthened the group's pursuit of the lean enterprise.

Once companies in the stream, including the team leader, accept a set of clear principles, the next step is mutual verification. The activities of each company must be transparent so that the upstream and downstream collaborators can verify that all tasks are being performed adequately. One way to do this is a continuing process "audit" similar in spirit to the audits companies currently perform on the quality assurance techniques of suppliers. Such audits must be conducted jointly and in both directions: customer-supplier and supplier-customer. This means the end of secrecy in product development and production operations and suggests the need to go even further with activity-based costing so that the indirect costs of all activities are fully understood and dramatically reduced.

The most difficult disputes between enterprise members will involve their respective productivity and creativity rather than their respective profit margins. Some members might say to another member, "Your profit margin is actually too low. Your costs are much too high because you failed to apply lean techniques in product development and production processes. We won't help pay for your inefficiency." Or they might say, "You seem unable to provide the next generation of technology for a key component system in our shared product. Address this issue or find a new enterprise!"

Proposals for virtual corporations, in which "plug-compatible" members of the value stream come and go, fail to grasp the massive costs of casual interactions. These arrangements are fine for nascent industries in which product specification and market demand are subject to dramatic and unpredictable change. But they are terrible for the vast majority of commercial activities.

The lean enterprise is also very different from the vertical keiretsu of Japan, whose members cement their relationships by taking equity stakes in each other. Unlike keiretsu members, participants in the lean enterprise must be free to leave if collaborators fail to improve their performance or refuse to reveal their situation.

Strategy for the Lean Enterprise

The companies joined in a lean enterprise must target the best opportunities for exploiting their collective competitive advantage. But their strategic thinking must also include a new element to complement and sustain the new concepts of careers, functions, companies, and the shared enterprise: how to find additional activities sufficient in magnitude to sustain the relationships that are the basis of superior performance.

We noted at the outset that, by its nature, the lean enterprise does more and more with less and less. This performance leap requires the continuing gung-ho involvement of every employee and allied company. All companies in a value stream must collectively determine how much labor, space, tooling, and time are necessary. Each member of the enterprise must then focus its activities by returning all employees who are not creating value to their home functions. It is impossible to implement and sustain a lean value stream with excess people, space, time, and tools.

Of course, unceremoniously dumping employees and allies as productivity gains are realized is the best way to ensure that such gains are not sustained. Employees will naturally place self-preservation above the value stream. In addition, companies that fire thousands of people run the risk of sparking a public backlash that could lead to greater government restrictions on their ability to shrink their workforces.

So how can companies avoid massive layoffs? One way is lowering prices by passing the cost savings on to the final consumer in order to increase sales or to grab share from less lean competitors. (Obviously, individual suppliers, especially in the West, now cannot dictate that their price reductions be passed on to final consumers. This is another reason the lean enterprise, which can make sure this happens, is so important.)

Companies must pursue every option for preserving jobs as they create lean enterprises.

Another way is speeding up product development to expand offerings in existing product families and to create new markets for core technologies.

Clearly, not every company in every enterprise can preserve all of its jobs. Some companies in mature industries may have to lay off workers or abandon suppliers. However, companies that sincerely and visibly explore all options for preserving jobs as they create lean enterprises will make unavoidable layoffs easier for employees to accept.

The Prize

A concerted effort by companies across the industrial landscape to embrace the lean enterprise *and* find new tasks for excess employees will be vastly superior to any industrial policy that governments devise. An economy dominated by lean enterprises continually trying to improve their productivity, flexibility, and customer responsiveness might finally be able to avoid the kind of social upheavals that have occurred when new production systems have rendered existing ones obsolete.

If this sea change in industrial practice comes to pass, most individuals, companies, and enterprises will prosper. Equally important, we will witness a productivity explosion, coupled with employment stability, that will provide the long-sought antidote to the economic stagnation plaguing all advanced economies.

Lucas: Undermined from Without and Within

BY IMPLEMENTING LEAN techniques, Lucas PLC, a British supplier of mechanical and electrical components to the automotive and aerospace industries, made great strides in improving product quality and on-time deliveries. But after about seven years, progress ground to a halt in some operations because key customers had not similarly adopted lean thinking. And other operations began to backslide as Lucas's plant managers and functional departments resisted changes that they saw as threats to their power.

Lucas was one of the first British companies to adopt lean techniques when it recruited University of Birmingham Professor John Parnaby in 1983 to head a new process-improvement function. Parnaby quickly introduced the concepts of the Toyota Production System throughout Lucas, with extremely promising initial results. For example, a Lucas aerospace-component plant halved its lead times and work-in-progress inventories, and a truck-component plant doubled its inventory turns and boosted the portion of orders delivered on time from 25% to 98%. Thanks to such improvements, Lucas began to overcome its reputation among customers as the "Prince of Darkness."

But problems soon emerged. An electrical-component factory that had embraced lean techniques, for example, found itself backsliding because big customers like Rover and Ford had not yet made their operations lean. As a result, these customers continued to place orders in an unpredictable fashion. To cope, the factory had to maintain relatively high inventories, a cardinal sin in lean production. True to form, workers began to rely on the inventories as a safety net, and the lean factory began to gain weight.

Within Lucas, the new process-improvement function was soon locked in a struggle with the traditional, vertical functions—marketing, product development, engineering, and production—over the former's efforts to improve efficiency. One plant installed a production line to manufacture a mechanical system in a continuous flow. But ignoring Parnaby's protests, the engineering function bought and installed some expensive, inflexible machines, which, as is typical of such equipment, were difficult to switch from making one type of component to making another. As a result, the plant had to revert to batch production, and inventories and inefficiencies quickly increased.

Internal conflict at Lucas was also evident at a plant for making truck components when the product-design function refused the advice of the process-management function. The latter developed a component that promised to be superior to competitors' offerings, but it turned out that the component couldn't be manufactured to the tolerances required. If a cross-functional design team including process management and production engineering had overseen the project, this folly could have been avoided.

Discouraged by all the battles within and without, Parnaby scaled back his efforts to institute lean thinking at Lucas. Hard hit by slumps in its key markets in the 1990s, Lucas has seen its profits wither, has suffered from management turmoil, and has dramatically shrunk its product offerings and slashed its payrolls. The company has also been a rumored takeover target. The person who must contend with these problems is George Simpson, who will assume the helm of Lucas in May. As the chairman of Rover, the British automaker, Simpson has used lean production to improve Rover's competitiveness dramatically. He will undoubtedly try to force Lucas to carry on the lean revolution it began over a decade ago.

Chrysler's Next Challenge: Building Lean Enterprises

AS WE WERE FINISHING our research for *The Machine That Changed the World* in early 1990, we decided to say as little about Chrysler as possible. We believed that the company's managers were brilliant at selling poor-quality products and terrible at product development, production operations, and supply-chain management. While Chrysler executives vowed that they were implementing lean techniques in each of these areas, we were highly skeptical.

We were spectacularly wrong. Chrysler actually was embracing lean production, and the company is now trying to turn the value chains it leads into lean enterprises. As Chrysler has worked toward this end, the conflicts between the needs of value streams and those of the individuals, functions, and companies that make up the streams have become fully apparent. Chrysler is beginning to realize that overcoming these obstacles is its next great challenge.

As part of Chrysler's move toward lean production, the company revamped its purchasing system and deployed cross-functional "platform" teams, each of which focuses on developing one line of cars or trucks. The platform teams have been a spectacular success in part because Chrysler appointed a traditional function head to lead each team in order to minimize process-function conflict. The head of purchasing, for example, also heads the small-car team. Therefore, if a function acts as a roadblock to one platform team, the team's leader can threaten to hold hostage the product under development by the offending function head's own team. We don't propose this as a model for other companies, but this approach has certainly ended Chrysler's long-standing functional feuding.

Thanks to a host of new products that command prices in the top range of their market segments and dramatic reductions in production costs due to better design, Chrysler will probably make as much money in 1994 as will all Japanese automakers combined. Moreover, the time that Chrysler requires to bring a product concept to market has been cut from 60 months in the 1980s to 31 months for the Neon, launched in January 1994. The number of full-time engineers involved in developing a new body and integrating the vehicle systems has gone from 1,400 to 700. And the enhanced manufacturability of the product has reduced the number of hours required to paint, weld, and assemble a vehicle from 35 to 22. Both the amount of time spent on final tinkering with the product in the early stages of production and the number of product recalls have also been slashed.

But such successes do not mean all is well. Most members of the platform teams have been permanently removed from their former functional "home," the body engineering department. Until recently, team members were content to be part of a process with clear and positive results. But they are now becoming anxious about their lack of a career path (these teams don't need layers of managers with fancy titles) and the dilution of their skills due to lack of communication with colleagues elsewhere in the company. Chrysler's challenge is to define a new career for these employees, which should involve alternating them between teams engaged in developing and making products and jobs where they can deepen their skills.

Such a solution would also address an emerging problem caused by the elimination of the body engineering department. While this department was a major roadblock for the company, its elimination has created a vacuum in functional expertise at a time when the auto industry is experimenting with new body technologies based on aluminum space frames with plastic or aluminum skins. Chrysler dares not fall behind in its fundamental technical capabilities but does not wish to send the advanced R&D function on excursions unrelated to the practical needs of the platform teams. The company, therefore, must redefine its engineering functions so that they support its key processes but still have a life of their own.

Chrysler also faces the challenge of redefining its supplier relations in order to create four lean enterprises: small cars, large cars, minivans, and trucks and Jeeps. The company has winnowed its supplier base from a chaotic mass of 2,500 in the late 1980s to a lean, long-term nucleus of 300. At the moment, suppliers love working for Chrysler, and for obvious reasons: the company's production volume is growing rapidly. Chrysler includes suppliers in development activities from day one and listens eagerly to their suggestions for design improvements and cost reductions. Chrysler has also replaced its adversarial bidding system with one in which the company designates suppliers for a component and then uses target pricing (figuring out how much consumers will pay for a vehicle and then working backwards to divvy up the costs and profits) to determine with suppliers the component prices and how to achieve them. Most parts are sourced from one supplier for the life of the product.

Despite these improvements, Chrysler still pays too much for most of its parts. The problem is not excessive supplier profit margins but that Chrysler, like most Western automakers, has not been successful in getting suppliers to implement lean techniques in ways that are best for the enterprise. In addition, Chrysler and its suppliers have yet to devise pain-sharing principles to keep their relationship from degenerating into an "every company for itself" battle in the next economic downturn.

Chrysler's management is energetically trying to address these problems. Indeed, Chairman Robert Eaton and President Robert Lutz have made it clear that Chrysler's main challenge in the 1990s is devising and perfecting its own lean enterprises.

Unipart: Turning Functions into Schools

BRITAIN'S UNIPART GROUP HAS gone further than most companies in turning its functions into schools as part of the company's effort to become lean. Unipart was created in 1987, when Rover sold a collection of disparate, highly autonomous functions to employees. Unipart then turned these functions into independent divisions, which included auto-parts manufacturing; ware-housing, distribution, marketing, and sales of Unipart's and others' auto components; information systems; and video production.

John Neill, Unipart's CEO, pushed each Unipart business to become lean on its own. But auto-parts manufacturing was clearly the most successful. Its plants that make fuel tanks and exhaust systems for cars, which learned lean techniques from Honda's and Toyota's British plants, won the U.K. Factory of the Year Award in 1989 and 1993.

When Neill decided that the auto-parts manufacturing business should teach the other businesses its secrets, he quickly realized that given their history of operating autonomously, this was much easier said than done. He also realized that if things did not change, Unipart would fail to leverage the knowledge of a practice leader, and, because the businesses were interdependent to a certain extent, the laggards would prevent the whole company from becoming as lean as possible.

To tackle these problems, Neill created "Unipart University." He made each business responsible for finding the best practice in its field, customizing it for Unipart, and then teaching it to the other businesses and their partners. In other words, each Unipart business, complete with its own "faculty," is a center of expertise. "Through this forum we share the best available learning with our colleagues," Neill says.

The Information Technology Faculty, which resides in the information-systems company, for example, is responsible for upgrading IT skills throughout Unipart. And the Industries Faculty, which resides in the manufacturing company, is playing the lead role in teaching its suppliers as well as the warehouse operation the process-management techniques it gleaned from Honda and Toyota. In the case of the warehouse operation, this entails teaching it how to work with its major suppliers so that together they can fill orders on time, which will enable the warehouse operation to cut its inventories.

The "deans" of the faculties, most of whom are the heads of the businesses, sit on the Deans Group, which steers the university, ensures that problems are discussed companywide, and initiates research on ways to solve them. The Deans Group recently charged two faculties with a critical task: researching how to select and develop leaders of self-managed, shop-floor teams. As part of that effort, the group from the industries and warehousing faculties visited Japan and the United States as well as Honda's and Toyota's British operations.

"Our vision," Neill says, "is to build the world's best lean enterprise. That means continuously integrating training, or should I say learning, into the decision-making systems of the company."

Originally published in March–April 1994
Reprint 94211

About the Contributors

CARLISS Y. BALDWIN is the William L. White Professor of Business Administration at Harvard Business School. Prior to her position at Harvard, she taught as an Assistant Professor at MIT's Sloan School of Management. She is currently involved in a multiyear project with Kim Clark that studies the process of design and its impact on the structure of the computer industry. Earlier projects have included investigating capital budgeting systems in large U.S. companies, and a study of the optimal methods of sale in corporate divestitures. In addition to research and teaching, Professor Baldwin serves as a Director of Country Curtains, Inc., and she was formerly the Director of the Federal Home Loan Division of Bank of Boston and served on the Economic Policy Advisory Board of the U.S. Council of Economic Advisors. She is the author of several publications including her most recent book, coauthored with Kim Clark, *Design Rules: The Power of Modularity.*

KIM B. CLARK is the Dean of the Faculty and the George F. Baker Professor of Administration at Harvard Business School. His most recent book, *Design Rules: The Power of Modularity*, is coauthored with Carliss Baldwin and focuses on modularity of design and the integration of technology and competition in industry evolution, with a particular focus on the computer industry. Earlier research has covered the areas of technology, productivity, product development, and operations strategy. He has published numerous articles in journals such as *Harvard Business Review*, *California Management Review*, *Management Science*, and *Administrative Science Quarterly*, and is the author or coauthor of seven books.

JEFFREY H. DYER is an Associate Professor of Management at the Marriott School, Brigham Young University, where he holds the Donald Staehli Chair in International Strategy. Prior to his BYU appointment, Dr. Dyer was a Professor in the management department at The Wharton School, University of Pennsylvania. His work experience includes five years as a Consultant and Manager at Bain & Company. His current research focuses on global strategy, strategic alliances, supplier management, and interorganizational learning. He is the author or coauthor of several articles that have appeared in publications such as *Strategic Management Journal*, *Harvard Business Review*, and *Academy of Management Review*. He also has a forthcoming book on supply chains entitled *Collaborative Advantage*.

MARSHALL L. FISHER is the Stephen J. Heyman Professor and Codirector of the Fishman-David Center for Service and Operations Management at The Wharton School at the University of Pennsylvania. He has consulted to a number of top companies, including Campbell Soup, General Motors, IBM, and Andersen Consulting, and he is a member of the National Academy of Engineering. His current areas of interest are supply chain management and retailing. In addition to his articles in *Harvard Business Review*, he has also published in *Operations Research*.

DONALD V. FITES served as Chairman and Chief Executive Officer of Caterpillar Inc. from June, 1990 until his retirement in February, 1999. His 42 years with Caterpillar include 16 years in overseas management positions as well as serving as Corporate Vice President, Executive Vice President, Director, and President and Chief Executive Officer. In addition to his continuing membership on Caterpillar's board of directors, he is also a Director of Mobil Corporation, Georgia-Pacific, AT&T, and Wolverine World Wide. He has received numerous awards including: the 1995 CEO of the Year by *Financial World Magazine*, the 1996 Salvation Army's William Booth Award, the 1998 Consumers for the World Trade Annual Award, the 1999 Executive of the Year by the Executives Club of Chicago, and the 1999 Creve Coeur Club of Peoria's Robert H. Michel Lifetime Achievement Award.

DANIEL T. JONES is a Professor of Management and Founder of the Lean Enterprise Research Centre at Cardiff University Business School in the United Kingdom. His main interests are the causes of differences in industrial performance and the transfer of a set of principles, called lean thinking, from Toyota to a wide range of industries across the globe. He is the coauthor of three books with Dr. James P. Womack: *The Future of the Automobile*, *The Machine that Changed the World*, and *Lean Thinking*.

NIRMALYA KUMAR is a Professor of Marketing and Retailing at the International Institute for Management Development (IMD) in Switzerland. Prior to joining IMD, he held appointments at Pennsylvania State University and Northwestern University's Kellogg Graduate School of Management. He has also held positions at Sara Lee Corporation in Chicago and Price Waterhouse in Calcutta, India. As a coach, consultant, seminar leader, and speaker on marketing strategy, branding, distribution, and retailing, he has worked with over 30 Fortune 500 companies in more than 20 different countries. He has published numerous articles in publications such as *Financial Times, Harvard Business Review, Journal of Marketing,* and *Academy of Management Journal.*

JOAN MAGRETTA is a consultant and writer based in Cambridge, MA. A former Partner at the management consulting firm of Bain & Company, she is a Contributing Editor of the *Harvard Business Review,* and winner of the McKinsey Award for 1998. Her latest book, *Managing in the New Economy,* is a collection of *Harvard Business Review* articles.

RICHARD NORMANN is the Founder and Chairman of SMG, a Scandinavian based company advising corporations, institutions, and regions on strategic renewal. He works across Europe and in the United States. He has served as a Visiting Researcher at the Harvard Business School and currently holds a guest professorship at the Copenhagen Business School. A Global Business Network member, he is the author or coauthor of several books on business and leadership including *Management for Growth* and *Service Management.* A new book about business concept innovation will be published in 2000.

RAFAEL RAMÍREZ is a Professor of Management at HEC, France's leading business school. He has served as consultant or management educator in 20 countries for the top management of corporations and public service institutions of 15 nationalities. His current research is centered on the design, organization, and management of coproducing value with customers, and on the relationship between values and value. Professor Ramírez has collaborated in different roles with SMG, a Swedish strategy consultancy, for 14 years. He is an elected individual member of Global Business Network, and is fluent in Spanish, English, and French.

JAMES P. WOMACK is the Founder and President of the Lean Enterprise Institute, a nonprofit education and research

organization chartered in 1997 to advance a set of ideas
derived from Toyota and now commonly known as lean production, lean thinking, and lean enterprise. LEI works jointly
with partner firms to create a tool kit for implementing lean
thinking in new areas such as health care, construction, raw
materials production, and distribution logics. Dr. Womack
has coauthored several articles and books with Daniel T.
Jones over the past 20 years. The most widely known are *The
Machine That Changed the World* and *Lean Thinking*.

Index

accurate response approach, 153–154

after-sales service, 161, 162

alliances
  new logic of value and, 204–208, 215–216
  retailer power and, 93

AMC. *See* American Motors Corporation

American industrial tradition, 228–229

American Motors Corporation (AMC), 67

Anheuser-Busch Companies, 108

Apollo computer, 13–15

architecture
  modularity and, 13–16, 21
  as term, 26n1

Asian companies. *See also* Japanese companies; supply chain management
  Li & Fung and, 35–36, 58–59

ATMs. *See* automatic teller machines

AT&T, 15

automatic teller machines (ATMs), 194–196

automobile industry
  modularity in, 6–7, 8–10
  parts-delivery systems in, 165
  retailer trust and, 97–98, 107
  supply chain strategy and, 140–141, 143

Baldwin, Carliss Y., 1–27

Baldwin, James W., 183–184

Bankers Trust Company, 11–12

bilateral communication, 107–108

borderless manufacturing. *See* dispersed manufacturing

business functions. *See also* cross-functional teams
  in American industrial tradition, 229
  in German industrial tradition, 228
  lean enterprise and, 225–226, 234–236, 248–250

business systems
  Danish pharmacies and,
    197–204
  at IKEA, 191–193
  and new logic of value,
    191–193, 197–204
buying cycle, and supply chain
    management, 40, 41–42

Campbell Soup Company,
    133–134, 144–146
career development, 225,
    231–233
cash, and supply chain man-
    agement, 51–52
Castaing, François, 65, 68, 74
category killers, 93
Caterpillar, dealer relationships
    at, 109, 113, 155–184
  backhoe loader business
    and, 170
  company size and, 165–166
  corporate turnaround and,
    156–157
  distribution system and,
    160–166
  D9L track-type tractor and,
    168–169
  general lessons from,
    158–160
  investment in maintenance
    of, 171–180
  making global connections
    and, 181–184
  Partners in Quality program
    and, 167–168
  strategic role of, 166–171

cells. *See* modularity
Century Products, 130–131
Chrysler Corporation, dealer
    relationships at, 98
Chrysler Corporation, supplier
    relationships at, 61–90
  changes in practices from
    1989 to 1994 and, 71
  Chrysler's turnaround and,
    64–65
  communication and, 80–82,
    85
  compared with Japanese
    keiretsu, 84–86
  coordination and, 80–82
  cross-functional teams and,
    69–70
  Dodge Ram truck and, 64
  impetus for change and,
    66–69
  leadership and, 65
  lean enterprise and,
    245–248
  LH program and, 67–69,
    71–73
  long-term commitments
    and, 83–84
  new model of, 69–84
  number of suppliers and, 85
  presourcing and, 70
  process characteristics and,
    71
  profits and, 80, 81
  relational characteristics
    and, 71
  results of partnership model
    and, 86–90

SCORE program and, 62,
73–80
target costing and, 70–73
Clark, Kim B., 1–27
communication
bilateral, 107–108
dealer relationships at
Caterpillar and, 159,
176–177
listening and, 77–78
supplier relationships at
Chrysler and, 80–82, 85
trust and, 80–82, 107–108,
176–177
Compagnie Générale des Eaux,
209–210, 212–217
company needs
Japanese industrial tradition
and, 229–231
lean enterprise and,
226–227
Compaq Computer Corpora-
tion, 99, 138
compensation, and manufacturer-retailer relation-
ships, 91–92, 159
competence and customer
development
Danish pharmacies and,
197–198
French concessionaires and,
208, 209–210, 212–217
competition
dealership support and,
175
in modular environment, 5,
12–16

new logic of value and,
196–197, 214–215
compliance, 52–53
computer industry
complexity and, 3–6
modularity in, 1, 2–6
supply chain strategy and,
141–142
consumers, and modularity in
use, 7. *See also* customer
relationships
continuity, and dealer relationships, 178–180
continuous replenishment program, at Campbell Soup,
134, 144–146, 147
coordination, and supplier
relationships, 80–82,
143–144
co-production of value. *See*
value constellation
costs
benefits of trust and, 101
diminishing returns from
reduction of, 143–144
inventory and, 138, 145
supplier partnerships at
Chrysler and, 87–89
supply chain functions and,
132
supply chain management
and, 42–43
courtesy, and manufacturer-
retailer relationships, 111
credibility, and reinvented
business systems, 204
Crédit Lyonnaise, 218

cross-functional teams. *See also* multifunctional teams
 at Chrysler, 69–70, 246–247
 lean enterprise and, 232, 234–235, 244, 246
 manufacturer-retailer relationships and, 114–115, 121–122
customer relationships. *See also* competence and customer development
 dealers as channels and, 158–159, 162–163, 166, 167, 199
 dealers as service providers and, 159
 dialogue between competencies and customers and, 197–198, 208, 209–210, 212–217
 at IKEA, 189–190
 importance of service and, 163–164
 innovation and, 203–204
 organization focused on, 44–47, 114–115
 resistance and, 203–204
 supply chain management and, 55
 surveys and, 167
 value creation by customers and, 185, 190, 196, 208
Cyrk (company), 49

Danish Consumer Council, 206
Danish Pharmaceutical Association, 199–201, 203, 204–208
Danish pharmacies, 186, 197–204
 alliances and, 204–208
 health care delivery and, 201–204
 strengths in network of, 199
dealerships. *See* Caterpillar, dealer relationships at; manufacturer-retailer relationships
decision making
 explanation to partners and, 110
 LH development at Chrysler and, 69
 supply chain management and, 58
Delphi Automotive Systems, 9
density, and value, 195
dependability, 97
design process. *See also* product development
 challenges of modularity for, 7–8
 dealer feedback and, 166–167
 modularity in, 1–2, 4–6, 17
 principle of modularity in, at IBM, 4
design rules. *See* visible information
discount supercenters, 93
dispersed manufacturing, 29–30, 33–34. *See also* supply chain management

characteristics of, 34–36
process involved in, 36–37
distribution systems. *See* Caterpillar, dealer relationships at; manufacturer-retailer relationships
distributive justice, 105–106
Dubinsky, Donna, 22, 23
due process. *See* procedural justice
Dyer, Jeffrey H., 61–90

economic factors, and dealer relationships, 157, 173–174
EDI links. *See* electronic data interchange links
educational programs
business functions and, 234–236, 248–250
manufacturer-retailer relationships and, 115–116
Ekornes, J.E. *See* J.E. Eckornes
electronic data interchange (EDI) links, 144
employees. *See also* individuals
alternating career paths and, 231–233
career development and, 225
lean enterprise and, 225, 231–233, 241–242
manufacturer-retailer relationships and, 114–115
modularity and, 19–20
emulator modules, 5

"encash," 51
engineering function, 234, 235–236
engineering, research, and development (ER&D) expenses, 87, 88
entertainment industry, 95–96
entrepreneurship, 17, 172
supply chain management and, 47–48, 51
equitability, and dealer relationships, 159
ER&D. *See* engineering, research, and development expenses
Eurogroup, 93
European Retail Alliance, 93
Europharm Forum, 206, 207
explanation, and manufacturer-retailer relationships, 110
"extended enterprise," 85. *See also* Chrysler Corporation, supplier relationships at

facilities expenses, 87
fairness. *See* procedural justice
familiarity, and manufacturer-retailer relationships, 110–111
family business. *See* continuity, and dealer relationships; Li & Fung; supply chain management
Federated Department Stores, 93

Fidelity, 11–12

financial services industry, 11–12

Fisher, Marshall L., 127–154

Fites, Donald V., 155–180, 183

Ford Motor Company, 83–84, 97–98

forward buying, 145

French concessionaires, 186, 208–219
  dialogue between competencies and customers and, 208, 209–210, 212–217
  history of concession system and, 217–219
  public services in France and, 210–212, 215

functional products, and supply chain strategy, 131–132, 133–135, 139, 143–148

functions. *See* business functions

Fung, Victor, 29–59

Fung, William, 31

furniture industry. *See* IKEA

Gardner, Glenn, 65, 68, 74

Générale des Eaux. *See* Compagnie Générale des Eaux

General Motors Corporation (GM), 9, 10, 74, 83–84, 98

German industrial tradition, 228

Goodyear Tire and Rubber Company, 99

gouging, and manufacturer-retailer relationships, 172–173

government policy
  concessionaire system in France and, 209–212
  Japanese industrial tradition and, 229–230
  regulation of Danish pharmacies and, 198, 200

Hawkins, Jeff, 21–23

health-care sector, in Denmark, 201–206. *See also* Danish pharmacies

heavy equipment industry, 158, 173–174. *See also* Caterpillar, dealer relationships at

hidden design parameters, 4–5, 21

Honda Motor Company, 66–67, 233, 249, 250

Hong Kong Trade Development Council, 31

IBM
  Central Processor Control Office, 4–5
  System/360 and, 4–5, 8, 11

IBS. *See* Inchcape Buying Services

IKEA, 186
  Business Service Department, 191

co-production of value at, 189–193

IKEA Engineering unit and, 191

integrated business systems at, 188–193

logistics system at, 191–193

new logic of value at, 193–197

store design and, 189–190

transformation at, 188–189

warehouse system at, 192

impartiality, and manufacturer-retailer relationships, 108–109

incentives

Chrysler's SCORE program and, 78, 84–85

at Li & Fung, 51

manufacturer-retailer relationships and, 91–92, 159

pricing and, 147

supply chain management and, 51

Inchcape Buying Services (IBS), 35

individuals

in American industrial tradition, 228–229

needs of, and lean enterprise, 225, 231–233, 241–242

industrial policy, versus lean enterprise, 222

industrial traditions, and lean enterprise model, 227–231

information economy, and supply chain management, 53–54

information hiding, principle of, 26–27n1

information technology (IT)

distribution system at Caterpillar and, 166, 181–184

new logic of value and, 193–195

supply chain management and, 56, 127, 129

information, visible versus hidden, 4–5. *See also* hidden design parameters; visible information

innovation

in functional products, 130–131

Li & Fung and, 59

modularity and, 5–6, 7, 16–17, 19

rate of new product introduction and, 139–143

supply chain strategy and, 130–131, 132–133, 134–143, 148–154

interdependence, effects of, 101–103

interfaces, 21

IT. *See* information technology

Japanese companies

after-sales service and, 161

distribution and, 160–162

Japanese companies *(continued)*
  Japanese industrial tradition and, 229–231
  keiretsu and, 63, 84–86, 240–241 (*See also* Chrysler Corporation, supplier relationships at)
  lean enterprise model and, 233, 237
  trust among auto dealerships and, 97–98
J.E. Ekornes (Norwegian manufacturer), 112, 123–125.
Jones, Daniel T., 221–250

keiretsu, 63, 84–86, 240–241
knowledge. *See also* competence and customer development; information technology
  dialogue between competencies and customers and, 208, 209–210, 212–217
  leaders as managers of, 2, 16–20
  needs of functions in lean enterprise and, 225–226, 248–250
  role of functions and, 234
Komoto, Makoto, 150
Kraft, 108–109, 114
Kumar, Nirmalya, 91–126

layoffs, avoidance of, 241–242

leadership
  business relationships as personal and, 177–178
  dealerships and, 176
  knowledge management and, 2, 16–20
  modular industries and, 2, 16–20
  turnaround at Chrysler and, 65
lean enterprise, 221
  Chrysler and, 245–248
  conflicting needs and, 221–222, 224–227
  industrial traditions and, 227–231
  Lucas PLC and, 243–245
  needs of companies and, 226–227, 229–231, 236–237
  needs of functions and, 225–226, 228, 229, 234–236, 248–250
  needs of individuals and, 225, 228–229, 231–233
  obstacles to, 223–224
  relationships among members of, 237–241
  strategy for, 241–242
  Unipart Group and, 248–250
  value of, 242–243
  versus virtual corporation, 223, 240
lean production, 222–223
Li & Fung, 29, 30–31. *See also* supply chain management changes at, 50–51, 57–59

development of, 32–34
global reach of, 38–39
organization at, 44–48
tradition of innovation at,
    59
venture capital involve-
    ments and, 49–50
Western business influence
    and, 57–59
Lopez, Jose Ignacio, 75, 114
Lucas PLC, 243–245
Lutron Electronics, 151
Lutz, Robert, 65, 68, 74–75, 248
Lyonnaise des Eaux Dumez,
    209–210, 212–217

*The Machine That Changed the
    World* (Womack and
    Jones), 221, 222, 245
Magna International, 10, 79–80
Magretta, Joan, 29–59
manufacturer-retailer relation-
    ships, 101–104. *See also*
    Caterpillar, dealer rela-
    tionships at
    benefits of trust in, 98–101,
        123
    characteristics of power ver-
        sus trust games in, 113
    creation of trust in,
        104–111, 159, 172–180
    effects of power exploitation
        in, 94–96
    gouging and, 172–173
    J.E. Ekornes and, 112,
        123–125

limits of trust in, 101–104
nature of trust in, 96–98
partner selection and, 112
Proctor & Gamble and Wal-
    Mart and, 101, 103–104,
    120–123
research on, 93–94
transition to trust in, 112–116
manufacturing
    dealer feedback and,
        166–168
    excellence in, 160
    modularity in, 1, 6–7, 8–10
        (*See also* dispersed man-
        ufacturing)
manufacturing program deliv-
    ery, 33
marketing
    dealer feedback and,
        168–169
    lean enterprise and, 234, 235
market mediation function,
    131–132, 138
Marks & Spencer, 41, 104,
    105–106, 107–108,
    109–111, 113–114
mass customization, 151–152
Matsushita Electric, 149, 230.
    See also National Bicycle
Matsushita-Kotobuki Electron-
    ics Industries (MKE), 24
May Department Stores Com-
    pany, 93
McDonald's Corporation, 104
megaformats, emergence of, 93
Mercedes-Benz, 9, 10, 104, 228

mergers and acquisitions, 93
metacompetence, 216
Mitsubishi Heavy Industries, 157, 161
Mitsubishi Motors Corporation, 68
MKE. *See* Matsushita-Kotobuki Electronics Industries
modularity, 1–27
    in automobile manufacture, 6–7, 8–10
    at Caterpillar, 164
    competition and, 5, 12–16
    in computer industry, 1, 2–6
    design challenges and, 7–8
    guide to, 20–21
    leadership challenges and, 16–20
    in manufacturing, 1, 6–7, 8–10
    in service industries, 1–2, 11–12
    in use, 7
modular suppliers, 6, 7, 9–10
multifunctional teams, 103–104, 226. *See also* cross-functional teams
multinational corporation. *See* supply chain management

National Bicycle, 149–152
Neill, John, 249, 250
Nissan Motor Company, 66, 235
Normann, Richard, 185–219

Obermeyer, Walter R., 152. *See also* Sport Obermeyer

operating framework, and modularity, 18–19
organization structure. *See also* lean enterprise
    dispersed manufacturing and, 30, 44–48
    matrix organization and, 232
    modularity and, 17–19
outsourcing. *See* modular suppliers

Palm Computing, 21–23
Panasonic, 150
Parnaby, John, 243, 244
partnership model. *See* Chrysler Corporation, supplier relationships at; manufacturer-retailer relationships; SCORE program
Partners in Quality program at Caterpillar, 167–168
parts-delivery system, at Caterpillar, 164–166
performance measurement, and manufacturer-retailer relationships, 115, 116–120
performance standards, and dealer relationships, 159, 175–176
Pharmaceutical Care concept, 201–204
Philip Morris Company, 116
physical supply chain function, 131–132, 138
Planning Perspectives, 83–84

plug-compatible modules, 5
policy consistency, and dealer
relationships, 159
political environment, and
Danish pharmacies,
207–208
power. *See also* manufacturer-
retailer relationships
disadvantages of reliance
on, 92–96
of manufacturers, 92–93,
94–96
of retailers, 92, 93
preproduction and launch
(PP&L) expenses, 87
presourcing, 70
Price, Barry, 72, 77
price promotions
"everyday low pricing" and,
104, 146–147
overuse of, 144–145
pricing. *See also* price promotions
Danish pharmacies and,
200
at Proctor & Gamble, 104
Pritchett, Lou, 121
procedural justice, 106–111
process audit, 240
process-management function,
236
Proctor & Gamble Company,
91, 92, 94
incentives at, 115
product strategy at, 142–143
relationship with Wal-Mart,
101, 103–104, 120–123

procurement costs, 89
product delivery cycle, 40–41
product design. *See* design process; modularity
product development. *See also*
design process
at Caterpillar, 168–171
at Chrysler, 67–69, 86–87
distribution considerations
and, 160
lean enterprise and, 235
product group managers,
52–53
production system, and modularity, 17–18
product life cycle, and supply
chain strategy, 131, 133
profitability
Chrysler and, 89–90
competence and customer
development and, 215
Prokesch, Steven E., 181–184
public services. *See* French
concessionaires
purchasing function, 234

quality, and dealer feedback,
167–168
Quantum Corporation, 23–25

Ramírez, Rafael, 185–219
reciprocity, and trust, 98
refutability, and manufacturer-
retailer relationships,
109–110
regulation, 198, 200
relationship managers, 115

relationships. *See also*
alliances; Caterpillar,
dealer relationships at;
Chrysler Corporation,
supplier relationships at;
customer relationships;
lean enterprise; manufac-
turer-retailer relation-
ships; supplier relation-
ships; value constellation
new logic of value and, 196,
204–208
supply chain management
and, 54–55, 58
reliability, 163–164
resident engineers, 80–81
respect, and manufacturer-
retailer relationships, 111
retailing, 41. *See also* Caterpillar, dealer relationships
at; manufacturer-retailer
relationships
Rover (British automaker), 245,
248
Royal Ahold, 115

SARP. *See* scale to assess
retailer performance
scale to assess retailer performance (SARP), 116–120
SCORE (Supplier Cost Reduction Effort) program, 62,
73–80
supplier rating system and,
78–80
Sears, Roebuck and Company,
101, 111

services
manufacturer-retailer relationships and, 95–96
modularity in, 1–2, 11–12
U.S. strengths in, 160
Sherwin-Williams Company,
111
Shih, Stan, 40
Shin Caterpillar Mitsubishi,
157
Sony Corporation, 95, 230
sourcing agent strategy, 32–33
Sport Obermeyer, 133–134,
152–154
Stallkamp, Thomas, 65, 74
standards
dealer relationships and,
159, 175–176
modularity and, 21
stock-outs, 122, 138, 152
strategy. *See also* modularity;
supply chain manage-
ment; supply chain strat-
egy
architect versus module-
maker, 13–16
new logic of value and,
196–197
subcontractors, versus modular suppliers, 6
subsystems. *See* modularity
Sun Microsystems, 14–16
supplier relationships. *See also*
Chrysler Corporation, supplier relationships at; supply chain management;
supply chain strategy

at Chrysler, 61–90, 247–248
cross-functional teams and,
    69–70
dedicated facilities and, 82
at IKEA, 190–191
long-term commitments
    and, 83–84
lower levels of supply chain
    and, 85
at Nissan, 239
presourcing and, 70
supply chain management
    and, 54–55
target costing and, 70–73
traditional approach to,
    62–63
supply chain management,
    29–59. *See also* dispersed
    manufacturing; supply
    chain strategy
buying cycle and, 40, 41–42
cash incentives and, 51–52
compared with traditional
    trading business, 32–34
delivery cycle and, 40–41
dispersed manufacturing
    and, 29–30, 33–36, 37
entrepreneurial approach
    in, 45–48
geographic issues and,
    46–47
information economy and,
    53–54
organization versus strategy
    in, 44–47
policy committee and,
    52–53

problems with supply
    chains and, 127–129
role of corporate center in,
    48
role of divisions in, 45–48
traditional trading relation-
    ships and, 54–55
value added by, 43–44, 45
supply chain strategy, 127–154.
    See also supply chain
    management
changes in product strategy
    and, 134–135
demand patterns and, 128,
    129–130, 136
formulation of ideal strategy
    and, 135–139
functional versus innovative
    products and, 128,
    130–139
functional products and,
    131–132, 133–135, 139,
    143–148
innovative products and,
    130–131, 132–133,
    134–143, 148–154
performance problems and,
    127–129
physical versus market
    mediation function and,
    131–132, 138
types of supply chain func-
    tions and, 131–132
support, and dealer relation-
    ships, 174–175

"tackling the soft $3," 42–43

target costing, 70–73, 238

targets, and SCORE, 78

teams. *See also* cross-functional teams; multifunctional teams
  LH development at Chrysler and, 68–69
  modularity and, 18–19

technological synergies, 214

telecommunications, 81–82. *See also* information technology

television networks, and manufacturer-retailer relationships, 95–96

time-sensitive products, and supply chain management, 40

Toyota Motor Corporation, 228, 230
  lean production and, 222, 243, 249, 250
  Lexus division, 106

Toys R Us, 31, 104

trading. *See* supply chain management

transaction costs, 89

trust. *See also* manufacturer-retailer relationships
  benefits of, 98–101
  creation of, 104–111, 159, 172–180
  distributor relationships at Caterpillar and, 161–162, 172–180
  exclusivity and, 103
  limits of, 101–104

long-term commitments and, 83–84
  nature of, 96–98
  relationships within lean enterprise and, 237–241

uncertainty
  acceptance of, 148–149
  avoidance of, 149–154
  innovative products and, 148–154
  modularity and, 17
  strategies for management of, 149

Unipart Group, 248–250

UNIX operating system, 14–15

use, modularity in, 7

value constellation. *See also* Danish pharmacies; French concessionaires; IKEA
  alliances and, 204–208, 215–216
  Danish pharmacies and, 186, 197–204
  French concessionaires and, 208–219
  IKEA and, 188–197
  new logic of value and, 193–197
  traditional notion of added value and, 186–187

value creation. *See also* value constellation
  by customers, 185, 190, 196, 208

manufacturer-retailer relationships and, 96
new logic of, 186–188
values, and partner selection, 112
value stream. *See also* lean enterprise
code of behavior within, 237–241
concept of, 223
management thinking and, 224
three needs in lean enterprise and, 224–227
virtual corporation, versus lean enterprise, 223, 240
visible information, 4–5, 6, 8, 18–19, 21
Volkswagen, 9–10, 12

Wal-Mart Stores, 91, 92, 101, 103–104
relationship with Proctor & Gamble, 101, 103–104, 120–123
Walton, Sam, 121
warehouse clubs, 93
WHO. *See* World Health Organization
Womack, James P., 221–250
World Health Organization (WHO), 206, 207

Zimmer, Steve, 85–86